ODD MAN OUT

A Motiveless Murder?

by Denise Beddows

Second edition

Published in 2018 by Misbourne Press

Copyright © Denise Beddows

Every effort has been made to contact the copyright holders of images and material used in this book and some sources did not wish to be acknowledged. However, where any omission has occurred, the author will gladly include acknowledgement in any future edition of the work.

A CIP catalogue record for this book is available from the British Library.

Cover design by Esther Kezia Thorpe.

'... Beddows paints a vivid picture of post-war Rawtenstall, and of the difficult lives of three women – a murder victim, her killer and the killer's lover. This is an exceptionally well researched account of a true crime and is a sensitive exploration of the difficult life and brutal death of this transgendered woman whom history has forgotten' – Murder Monthly.

'... another fascinating piece of research by the author of 'Running with Crows – The Life and Death of a Black and Tan'. In her latest book, 'Odd Man Out', Denise Beddows relates the intriguing but surprisingly under-reported case of Margaret 'Bill' Allen, Britain's only transgendered killer. This beautifully written account of a long-forgotten murder and execution highlights the shortcomings in the police investigation and leads us through the life and devastatingly sad fate of this tragic figure. It is particularly moving to read of the effects Allen's execution had on others and to know what happened next to all those involved.' – 'Bloggs on True Crime'.

'An extraordinary book ... well written, absorbing, thought provoking.' – Frost Magazine

ACKNOWLEDGEMENTS

I should like to express my extreme gratitude to Kathy Fishwick, author, historian and volunteer with the Rossendale Civic Trust, for her kind input, for giving me the benefit of her local knowledge and for checking my facts. I am indebted to Kathy and the Trust for kindly granting me permission to use some of their images. Sincere thanks also to Thomas Fishwick for the benefit of his local knowledge and his technical expertise in scanning images for me; to Ron Simpson for 'rescuing' the portrait of Nancy Chadwick; to Steve Yates for his photo of Margaret's house; to Peter Fisher for use of some of his amazing collection of images, and to Darrell Flood, Renee Hampson and some other lovely local folks who did not wish to be named, for sharing their information, images and recollections, all of which confirmed my impressions of the main characters in this true and tragic story.

'Murderers are so often ordinary people caught on the wrong foot,' – Albert Pierrepoint, Britain's official executioner [1932-1956].

CONTENTS

INTRODUCTION

Sunday 16 January 1955 was a bitterly cold day in Lancashire. Britain was in the grip of weather conditions which the press would dub 'The Big Freeze'. The temperature had dropped to four degrees below freezing – the lowest in thirty years – and northern counties were enduring intense blizzards. Up in the Pennines, motorists were stranded in their vehicles whilst, further north still, the RAF was dropping supplies to farmers trapped by thirty-foot snowdrifts.

Meanwhile, one Lancashire housewife was at home preparing Sunday lunch. Having banked up her fire to ward off the exceptional chill, she was preparing her vegetables whilst listening to 'The Billy Cotton Band Show' on the wireless. A sudden knock at the front door, however, heralded unexpected visitors. A man and a woman, both in their mid-thirties, stood on the doorstep.

'Annie Cook?' the man enquired.

The housewife's face fell. Annie – whose surname was no longer Cook – blanched as she wondered how the couple had tracked her down. She supposed they must be journalists on the hunt for a story for the Sunday newspapers. She had little doubt they were here to rake up an incident which had occurred six years earlier; an incident which had caused her much pain.

Annie's first instinct was to close the door. However, her callers quickly assured her they were not tabloid hacks but serious authors who were researching, for purposes of comparison, the cases of nine women executed for murder. They persuaded her that, although they were interested to discuss her relationship with one of those women, they would not disclose her current identity or her whereabouts in their planned book.

There must indeed have been something reassuring in the manner and appearance of the pair, and Annie must have been impressed that they had travelled from London in such atrocious weather to interview her. It may also have been that her good nature would not allow her to turn away two chilled strangers into a worsening blizzard. Whatever the reason, with some trepidation, she invited them in. Spreading sheets of newspaper on the linoleum to absorb the slush from their boots, she ushered them into her parlour and went to put the kettle on.

It was not just the north which was experiencing extremes of weather that day. At the very moment when Annie's visitors were sipping their tea up in Lancashire, some two hundred miles further south, light levels suddenly dropped and it became pitch dark in the middle of the day. This daytime darkness was alarming to Londoners who, having experienced the horrors of the Blitz, were now in the grip of The Cold War with its ever-present threat of sudden nuclear annihilation. Unsurprisingly therefore, many in the capital feared this midday blackout might be the result of a nuclear attack.

Anxious Londoners jammed the press switchboards, thousands of 999 calls were logged and Prime Minister Winston Churchill ordered an immediate situation report. However, it transpired that there was no sinister reason for the sudden darkness. It was simply an accumulation of polluted air, blown down onto the capital by the same strong north westerly winds which were depositing snow on the nation's northern counties.

And, so it was, that on this, the oddest of January days – which, incidentally, was Annie's 39th birthday – that she gradually revealed her side of a surprisingly under-reported story. Comfortable in the presence of her visitors, romantic novelist Renée Huggett and Paul Berry, a feminist sympathiser and pacifist, Annie gradually revealed her inside knowledge of a very unusual murder. That murder was one perpetrated by an unlikely killer upon an unlikely victim. The killer was Margaret Allen, Annie's best friend and, perhaps, her lover.

Despite what we shall see was the obvious eccentricity of the victim and the unconventional nature of the perpetrator, as well as the sensational brutality of the killing, this case was labelled 'a motiveless murder' and it has sunk with quiet anonymity into the dusty annals of crime. The fact that greater detail of the case did not make it into the popular press of the time is largely due to the reluctance of the accused to say why she did it. She did not offer a spirited defence and nor did she express any remorse. She declined to appeal against her conviction and death sentence but, instead, went calmly and resignedly to the scaffold.

The official files in this case being disappointingly thin, and the press reports being few, superficial and inaccurate, I make no excuse, therefore, for my frequent references to the interviews recorded by authors Huggett and Berry. Their enquiries were conducted only six years after the incident and whilst Annie was still alive. Though I am grateful for their invaluable impressions, I reserve the right to disagree with some of their conclusions. Also, Huggett and Berry did not have access to the original evidential statements, whereas I did.

Huggett and Berry would describe Margaret as *'the assertive, extremely masculine type of lesbian'*. Others commenting on the case in academic dissertations or in articles featured in lesbian literature would cite her execution as an example of society's prejudice against the homosexual woman. However, Margaret was not a lesbian. She believed she was a man born into the body of a woman and, as such, she had all the emotions and inclinations of a man. In adulthood, she chose to dress as a man and she insisted on being addressed as 'Bill'. Because of this, she attracted derision, verbal abuse and even assault from some sections of her community. She was what nowadays would be termed transgendered, although, during her lifetime, her anomalous condition was neither widely recognised nor given a name.

Some commentators on the case, though these are few in number, have referred to Margaret Allen as 'she', others as 'he', and at least one writer has confused the issue somewhat by randomly mixing both gender pronouns. To avoid confusion, and for ease of visualising someone who was in all physical respects female, albeit by instinct a male, I shall – with great apology to Margaret – use the female pronouns. Since we are outsiders looking into her world, I shall show Margaret as her community saw her, rather than as she preferred to see herself, and I shall also refer to her using her given, rather than chosen name.

I do so because I feel this will illustrate her predicament more keenly. Simply writing of 'Bill and Annie' as 'he' and 'she' would, I feel, cause the reader to visualise theirs as an ordinary heterosexual relationship which, owing to society's attitudes and the inadequacy of the medical profession back then, it could not be. Nowadays, it seems, Margaret might be labelled a 'transman' but such terminology was not used during her lifetime and so this seems to me to be inappropriate in a retrospective account.

I came upon details of the case by chance but immediately it resonated with me for two reasons, the first being my childhood memories of Sunday escapes from our own grey, working class area of Manchester up to the green and beautiful Rossendale Valley. Secondly, it chimed with my late mother's account of her service as a wartime bus conductress in Lancashire, since this was also Margaret Allen's chosen wartime occupation.

My late mother was an avid follower of the tabloid press reporting of murders and executions and she could recount in great detail every single case of the twentieth century. For example, she had an encyclopaedic knowledge of the crimes of wife-killer Hawley Harvey

Crippen; John George Haigh the acid bath murderer, and the tragic Ruth Ellis. Oddly, however, she never once mentioned the case of executed fellow bus conductress Margaret Allen. When, relatively recently, I learned of the case, naturally my curiosity was piqued.

My interest in researching the case stemmed from the apparent lack of any motive for the brutal killing of one woman by another who scarcely knew her victim. My greatest challenge was that the limited amount of detail which did appear in the press was frequently contradictory or incorrect. However, the scant official files revealed that a significant amount of critical evidence had been suppressed, and so I felt the case cried out for re-examination. The story of Margaret 'Bill' Allen and its tragic conclusion may well augment the conversation society nowadays is having about transgenderism and the treatment of transgendered individuals.

The combination of a victim and killer both described as 'abnormal' – the one painted an oddly eccentric miser, and the other inaccurately described as a lesbian – promised to be an intriguing story, but one which I have sought to explore with sensitivity, rather than sensationalism. This is an account of a marginalised and intensely lonely soul, someone who, by all accounts, was a very kind and likeable person but who, in the final years of her life, found herself sorely in need of friendship and love. This tragic tale could have had a happy ending, had Margaret not encountered a major obstacle in the way of her happiness.

As we approach the 70th anniversary of Margaret Allen's execution, I wanted to try and identify her real motive for committing this allegedly purposeless murder, to assess whether justice was served by inflicting the death penalty upon her, and to consider whether her life and the verdict in her case might have been any different had these events taken place in today's world. My main aim in writing this book, therefore, is to endeavour to make sense of a seemingly senseless crime. I hope also, in what I would like to think is an era of greater understanding, if not acceptance, to give a voice to an executed woman who chose to say very little about herself or her crime but went quietly and with dignity to the gallows.

Denise Beddows
2018

Chapter 1 – The Murder

'Drama descended on Rawtenstall with the discovery early last Sunday morning of the body of an elderly woman in Bacup Road near to Fall Barn Fold. She had been battered to death.' – The Bacup Times, Saturday 4 September 1948.

In the early hours of Sunday 29 August 1948, the body of an elderly woman was found, brutally beaten to death and laid out on the carriageway of a main road in the Lancashire mill town of Rawtenstall. The woman had been beaten about the head numerous times with a heavy object. In fact, the skull had partly caved in, suggesting a frenzied attack with considerable anger or desperation behind it.

The killing aroused curiosity and consternation in equal measure because, somewhat surprisingly perhaps, it was the town's first ever recorded murder. Townspeople feared there must be some outsider, probably a big brute of a man, roaming the streets with murderous intent and seeking out the vulnerable. Just three days later, however, to everyone's surprise, a short, middle-aged local woman was arrested and charged with the killing.

There were more surprises in store when it emerged that the deceased and her killer had barely known each other. No clear motive would be established for this savage yet seemingly senseless killing. The only common factors linking murderer and victim were that both were

1

well known locally and each, in her own way, was considered to be quite odd, indeed, some would say 'abnormal'.

The locus

Rawtenstall is situated in the Rossendale valley, an area of outstanding natural beauty. The town grew up alongside one of the significant rivers which irrigate the region. Local place names, mainly of Anglo-Saxon origin, mostly reflect geographical features. 'Clough', for example, indicates a wooded river gorge whilst 'fold' suggests the location of a sheep fold or ox stall.

The river in question, and it will feature in the murder case, is the Irwell. Rising as springs just north of what is now the town of Bacup, the Irwell had provided the area's early inhabitants, mainly foresters, with a great bounty of salmon and roach. Its tributaries watered the meadows where sheep and cattle grazed, facilitating the production of wool and also butter and cheese for the domestic market. The fast-flowing Irwell, together with the dampness of the local climate, would later prove conducive to the domestic cotton industry. Indeed, the river was the reason the Industrial Revolution came to Rossendale and turned small settlements into towns.

Lancashire already had a thriving domestic woollen industry by the time raw cotton imports began arriving at Liverpool from America. Those locals who were already skilled in spinning and weaving wool provided a ready workforce for the new cotton mills. The damp climate prevented the cotton thread from drying out and snapping when spun under tension, and Lancashire's widespread coal supplies fed the steam-powered looms as the mechanised industrial age got under way. The increased demand for raw cotton supplies for the mills also brought the railway to Rawtenstall, and purpose-built sidings ran right up into some of the mills' unloading bays.

As well as the area having a favourable climate, the fast-flowing Irwell provided water for the manufacture and washing of cotton. Dye works and other related manufactories quickly sprang up along the Irwell's banks and these, too, provided work for men and women from all over this and other counties. Rawtenstall's industries would even attract workers – Margaret Allen's own father amongst them – from as far afield as famine-prone Ireland. The towns of Bacup, Rawtenstall, Ramsbottom and Bury grew up along the Irwell, and the river's lower reaches formed a natural boundary between the cities of Manchester and

Salford before, from the 1890s onward, being subsumed into the mighty Manchester Ship Canal.

Though water extraction and industrial pollution had slowly reduced the volume and fertility of the Irwell, from 1874 a thriving shoe and slipper manufacturing industry provided employment for thousands of Rossendale workers, including, at one time, Margaret Allen. The industry supplied footwear to the entire British Empire, and led to Rossendale being dubbed *The Golden Valley*. Rossendale's woollen goods, too, were exported around the globe, and stone from Rossendale quarries was used to build London's Trafalgar Square and other major buildings in the capital. The people of the district were hard-working, respectable and proud, both of their reputation and their industrial output.

The largely working-class population of Lancashire towns such as Rawtenstall proved susceptible to the growing Methodist movement, which preached that – in the eyes of God at least – the working classes were deemed equal to the wealthy local mill owners who gave them employment. John Wesley himself came to preach in the valley in 1747 and the Temperance Movement also took firm root here. Temperance bars, selling locally produced soft drinks such as Sarsaparilla and Dandelion & Burdock, became popular and, unlike the inns and public houses, were granted licences to dispense their beverages on Sundays. Fitzpatrick's, England's very last remaining temperance bar, established in 1871, still operates in Rawtenstall.

In the mid twentieth century, Rawtenstall was a town still dominated by sturdy mills with tall chimneys; a town of imposing stone churches and other fine buildings, such as the Carnegie library, the court house and the town hall. Some of the grander houses on the town's outskirts, set in rolling parkland, were the homes of those local families which had risen to become wealthy mill owners. The majority of residents, however, lived in more modest terraced houses in crowded streets, many of which were named in honour of those mill owners. Street names such as Whittaker, Hardman, Kay and Ashworth reflected the glory days when wool spelled wealth and cotton was 'king'.

Despite the wealth generated by the town's industries, many of the terraced houses lacked even the most basic of sanitation. Though most of the residents had access to at least a single cold tap, many would still have to use communal toilet blocks. Dank and airless cellar dwellings in the town were occupied mainly by the elderly poor right up until the 'slum clearance' demolition of the 1960s and 70s. This was the world inhabited by Margaret and her victim.

Still recovering from the horrors and privations of World War Two, the Rawtenstall of 1948 was, nevertheless, a peaceable and conservative industrial town, albeit rendered a little drab and weary by wartime neglect. Indeed, the war had left all of Britain virtually bankrupt and had severely depleted the nation's food stocks, so nationwide food shortages were common. In particular, imported commodities such as sugar were in short supply, owing to the destruction of commercial shipping. Sugar, too, will play a part in this tragedy. Food, clothing and petrol rationing was still in force in 1948, and the townspeople obtained their food coupons from the town's food office before exchanging them and their hard-earned cash for groceries at local stores such as Melia's or the Maypole.

Like Methodism, the Labour movement, too, had found a natural home in the Rossendale Valley, where, in 1948, people were beginning to benefit from the Labour Government's new national health, pensions and public assistance provisions. Such benefits were a boon to single women like the alleged killer and her victim, neither of whom had a working man to support them.

The people of Rawtenstall were surprisingly law-abiding. Crime levels in the town were comparatively low and mostly involved petty theft and assaults. In fact, no murder had ever been recorded in Rawtenstall, aside from a single case, almost a hundred years earlier, of infanticide and suicide. In 1853, the depressive young wife of a drunkard had, out of despair, cut her own throat and that of her baby. To the good people of Rawtenstall, therefore, murder was something which happened elsewhere, not here.

Murder was not unknown in the wider district, however. Indeed, just three months before the Rawtenstall murder, just ten miles distant in the town of Blackburn, over in the neighbouring Ribble Valley, there had been a most horrific killing. June Ann Devaney was a little girl just four weeks short of her fourth birthday when she was abducted from a hospital ward, raped and murdered. The case was notable, not just for its brutality and the age of the victim, but for the fact that it generated, for the first time ever, mass fingerprinting of an entire community. On 13 August 1948, Peter Griffiths, a 22-year-old Blackburn man, a former soldier with an alleged family history of schizophrenia, was arrested for the child's murder.

4

The 1944 disappearance of six-year-old Sheila Fox from Farnworth, Bolton, however, was never solved, and Rawtenstall had also suffered the loss of two of its own children during the war. Jack Hitchen and Fred Williams, two thirteen-year old boys from the Deanwater area, one of whom had a blind mother, had gone into the old mine workings looking for a potential shelter for that lady in the event of further enemy air raids. The boys had never been seen again, however, and widespread searches of the mines and the surrounding area had failed to find either the boys or any clues as to their disappearance.

After the killing of little June Devaney, local people began to wonder if there might be a connection between her murder and the disappearance of little Sheila Fox and the Deanwater boys. Following Griffiths' arrest, there was understandable disquiet in Rawtenstall over the numbers of battle-hardened soldiers who were still encamped just outside the town awaiting demobilisation. Might there be another Peter Griffiths at large? Some were reassured by the thought that what had happened to the little girl had happened in another town in another valley. Surely no grisly murder could ever happen over here, not in peaceful Rawtenstall, not in *The Golden Valley*?

The discovery

The body of the woman was found lying in the carriageway on the south side of the Bacup Road, a major thoroughfare linking the towns of Rawtenstall and Bacup. The discovery was made just before 4 am that Sunday by a busload of around twenty Rawtenstall Corporation Bus Company drivers and conductors, making their way home from an all-night union meeting which had commenced around midnight. The reason the men were meeting at such a late hour was that this was the only time the entire workforce would be available.

Some newspapers would report that the meeting had taken place at a sports club, others that it was held in the bus shed, but some locals remember it as having been held in the town hall's council chamber. Rawtenstall Corporation ran both the town hall and the bus company so this is feasible. Whatever the location of the meeting, at its conclusion some of the busmen had set off home on foot whilst others, who lived a little further afield, were heading home on a number forty-six bus, and were being driven east along the Bacup Road towards Waterfoot.

The driver of the bus, 48-year-old Waterfoot resident Herbert Beaumont, confirmed he had driven along that same stretch of road going to the meeting earlier that Saturday night, at around 11.55, and had seen nothing in the road then. On leaving the meeting at around 3.55 am on the Sunday morning, as he reached the junction of the Bacup Road and Fall Barn Fold, he had spotted what he had first taken to be a long sack left in the middle of the road and he had braked hard.

Beaumont and some of his fellow busmen had alighted, intending to remove the obstruction. To their horror, they discovered it was the body of a woman, lying face down with her head pointing towards the centre of the road and her coat collar pulled up to partly obscure her bloodied head. It was obvious that the woman was dead and, initially, the men assumed this must have been the result of a hit-and-run traffic accident.

Another of the busmen, sharp-eyed driver Joe Unsworth, observed that, although the woman's skull appeared to have been caved in, there was very little blood around. Suspecting, therefore, that the woman had been killed elsewhere, he remarked to his colleagues *this looks like a put-up job'*. Leaving Beaumont and the other busmen standing guard, he ran to the bus station and telephoned the police.

Police Constable Stanley Marsden was soon on the scene and, by first light, he had called out a local doctor and alerted Police County Headquarters at Preston. At 4.15 am, only twenty minutes after the body's discovery, local physician Dr Frederick Percival Kay arrived to examine the deceased in situ. Dr Kay's house and surgery were just five minutes' walk away, at the corner of Bacup Road and Greenbank Street. This probably explains why, in the days before specialist police forensic surgeons, Constable Marsden chose to summon him specifically.

Dr Kay declared the woman dead – a fact which, of course, was plainly obvious to all but, even today, no police officer is allowed to assume death, not even in cases where a head has been separated from its body by a mile or two. A qualified medic must always be summoned to certify that death has occurred.

Noticing at least one deep laceration on the skull, Dr Kay expressed his doubts that she had been run over. He estimated the woman had been dead around eight to ten hours, putting the time of death as between six o'clock and eight o'clock the previous (Saturday) evening.

The spot where the body was found was on the south side of the carriageway just a few feet from the front door of number 137 Bacup Road, and there were bloody drag marks on the pavement outside number 137. What Dr Kay did next is decidedly odd. Instead of cordoning off the scene to preserve it, Dr Kay had the body dragged all the way across the Bacup Road and placed on the pavement on the opposite (north) side of the road whilst a mortuary vehicle was awaited.

The police report, drafted later, would state that the body was found twenty-seven feet away from number 137, but this is incorrect. Twenty-seven feet is more likely to have been the distance from 137 to that spot to which Dr Kay had ordered the body moved.

Why he did not simply have the body moved a few feet onto the nearest bit of pavement is not clear. This may suggest that the good doctor's judgement was not entirely sound, or that, having been aroused from his slumber so early on a Sunday morning, he was not thinking clearly.

137 Bacup Road. The darkened area of the roadway is where the body was found. The photo was taken from the opposite pavement, to which the body was removed. The front door is that of 137 and just to the left is the scullery window. The arrow slit window belongs to the adjacent property, the entrance to which is just around the corner. (With kind permission of The National Archives)

Detective Sergeant John George Thompson had also attended the scene where he, too, recorded that, despite multiple head injuries and the deceased's scalp being saturated with blood, there was indeed very little blood spilled on the carriageway, though a little had pooled in the gutter.

By 9 am, Detective Constable Harold Rowbottom of the Preston Forensic Laboratory was also examining the scene and he took away for testing samples of ashes found in the street, as these were believed to have fallen from the clothing of the deceased woman.

Initial enquiries

CID officers did not normally work weekends or bank holidays, but 42-year-old Detective Chief Superintendent John Woodmansey of Preston CID was called at home that Sunday and quickly travelled over to Rawtenstall to take charge of the investigation. His boss, Assistant Chief Constable Albert Edward Waddington was also contacted. Perhaps fearing that the county's latest murder investigation might require the same massive effort the Blackburn killing had needed, and so might be beyond the capabilities of the Lancashire detectives, Waddington wasted no time in seeking assistance from his contacts in the Metropolitan Police at New Scotland Yard.

This was not the first time that Woodmansey, a big Yorkshireman, had been assigned their help. Four months earlier, two young boys had been assaulted by a man with a knife over in Farnworth, Bolton. One boy had escaped his attacker's clutches but the other, eleven-year-old Jack Quentin Smith, had been sexually assaulted and murdered. Scotland Yard's Detective Chief Inspector Capstick, a man famed for his ingenuity and hard-line tactics in solving murders, had been despatched to Lancashire to help Woodmansey.

Convinced that Peter Griffiths, the Blackburn man who had killed little June Devaney, was also responsible for Jack Smith's murder, Capstick had interviewed Griffiths in prison. However, despite Capstick's protracted and heavy-handed interrogation, Griffiths went to his death denying he had ever killed anyone other than June Devaney. In fact, the killing of Jack Quentin Smith is another case which remains unsolved to this day.

If Woodmansey resented Scotland Yard men again being involved in one of his cases, he does not appear to have shown it. Indeed, it was quite common for Scotland Yard officers' assistance in solving murders to be sought by regional police forces. This did not necessarily

8

reflect any lack of confidence on the part of regional police chiefs, but rather the fact that calling in Scotland Yard at a very early stage meant the Metropolitan police would pay their officers' travel and accommodation expenses. Thus, the regional force got extra and experienced man-power at no extra cost. If the regional force did not ask for their help until a later stage in the investigation, however, then the regional force would be expected to foot the bill for the Yard men's attendance.

In the Rawtenstall case, of course, the basic footwork would be undertaken immediately by the Lancashire constables. By eight o'clock that Sunday morning, uniformed police officers were conducting house-to-house enquiries around the locality. More uniformed officers were drafted in from around the county, and gum-booted sappers from the nearby army camp had already set about dredging the Irwell, which ran behind the nearby houses, parallel to the Bacup road. Since no handbag or purse was found with the body, robbery was suspected and so the soldiers were hoping to find the deceased's belongings and anything which might have been the murder weapon.

A police blood hound was also brought in to assist with the search and, that afternoon, a string shopping bag and handbag were spotted in the river by the weir at Fall Barn. These were suspected of having belonged to the dead woman. By a quarter past three that afternoon the body had been positively identified by the deceased's nephew as being that of 68-year-old Nancy Ellen Chadwick, who lived at 81 Hardman Avenue on Rawtenstall's Hall Carr Estate, approximately half a mile from where she was found.

By then the area was swarming with newsmen and cameramen from around the county, from the city of Manchester and the neighbouring county of Yorkshire. Their ranks quickly swelled as the national newspapers got wind of the story. The Sunday staff on duty at the local telephone exchange soon found their wires jammed by reporters trying to file copy.

At seven o'clock that Sunday evening, ACC Waddington called a press conference at Rawtenstall's substantial courtroom – the largest room in the town and the only one capable of accommodating all the pressmen. Waddington outlined what was known thus far about this possibly suspicious death. He asked the newsmen to publicise his appeal for anyone with knowledge of the deceased's last movements to come forward. There was, however, no immediate response to this appeal.

Although news of the woman's death had begun to spread far and wide beyond the town, the Lord's day was widely observed in Rawtenstall and so most of the townsfolk had attended church then returned to their homes. That summer had been disappointingly cold and rainy and there were few locals out on the streets that day. The few hardy walkers who were braving the wet and slippery slopes of the Rossendale Valley were unaware of what had transpired down in the town. In fact, despite the national publicity given to the discovery, the majority of Rawtenstall residents would not learn of the incident until reading of it in their newspapers on the Monday morning.

Initial press reports described the dead woman as being five feet two inches tall,[1] of medium build with dark brown hair turning grey. When found, she was wearing a grey coat with two large buttons on the front, a brown woollen dress, brown stockings, pale green ankle socks and black plain shoes. The press reported Nancy Chadwick's home as being in Rehoboth Street, Rawtenstall, though this seems to have been incorrect. For the previous two to three years, Nancy Chadwick had been living at 81 Hardman Avenue and, for some years before that, she had lived on Mount Pleasant. This was just one of the numerous inaccuracies that would appear in the press.

At a second press conference held just two hours after the first, ACC Waddington made a dramatic announcement. He advised that Blackburn Pathologist Dr Gilbert Bailey's findings, following a full post mortem examination, confirmed Nancy's head injuries were unlikely to be result of a traffic accident and that foul play was indeed suspected. This was now being pursued as a murder enquiry. This did not come as a surprise to the assembled journalists, however, as, doubtless, the local police had already tipped off the press about the likelihood of this being a murder. The pressmen would not have travelled in such numbers from neighbouring counties to report on a mere hit and run case. It was common back then for the police to issue tip-offs to the press, usually in return for 'a drink'.

Although full details of Dr Bailey's report were not disclosed at this time, the police had full knowledge of these and, in particular, they were aware of the presence on the body of ashes which were described by DC Rowbottom as being *of the same type as one would find in a domestic grate'*.

---

[1] A later report would state she was five feet four inches tall.

One witness who now came forward was another bus company employee, 31-year-old conductor James Arthur Marshall. He confirmed he had walked past the spot just twenty minutes before the body's discovery, en route to his home on Hardman Avenue, the same street in which the deceased had lived. He had been accompanied by colleagues George Aldous, William Ball, Thomas O'Brien, Harry Trickett, Leslie Crook, Edward Turner and James Lee. Walking four abreast along the Bacup Road, the men had seen nothing unusual, and certainly no body in the road. The statements of these men were helpful in establishing a very narrow time frame – roughly between 3.40 and 3.55 am – during which the body had been placed in the road.

Already travelling north on the overnight train from London into Manchester were Scotland Yard Detectives Chief Inspector Bob Stevens and his colleague Sergeant Campbell. They arrived in Rawtenstall on the Monday morning and immediately offered their assistance to Detective Superintendent Woodmansey. The Scotland Yard men's first suggestions were for urgent radio appeals to be relayed and messages to be flashed on local cinema screens, asking for information on the dead woman's movements in the hours leading up to her death.

Witnesses now began coming forward to offer information about their last sighting of Mrs Chadwick. Locals who knew the deceased volunteered their opinions on the sort of person she was and speculated on what, in their opinion, might have prompted the murder. The general consensus of local opinion about Nancy Ellen Chadwick was that she was a most peculiar woman – some would say 'abnormal'. This was an adjective that would also be applied to another local woman, when the finger of suspicion began to point in one particular direction.

Dr Kay's house, Bacup Road
(author's photo)

81 Hardman Avenue, home to Nancy
Chadwick and Paddy Whittaker, as
seen today. (Author's photo).

Chapter 2 – The Victim

'My aunt has been abnormal for as long as I have known her ...' –
William Barnes, nephew of the deceased.

As with any murder case where the killer's identity is not immediately known, the police first focused their enquiries on the deceased.

Nancy Chadwick was born Nancy Ellen Barnes on 10 August 1880 in Haslingden. For some reason, however, she was not baptised until the age of four. She and her elder brother, five-year-old James Greenwood Barnes, and younger sister, Annie Barnes aged two, were all baptised on the same day, 24 August 1884. The family were then living at Higher Hud Hey, Haslingden.

Nancy was the second of six children, and the first daughter born to George Henry Barnes and Frances Ellen, née Barker. Nancy's father was a loom overseer in a cotton mill. Sadly, in 1888, 32-year-old Frances died giving birth to her sixth child. Nancy was just eight years old when she lost her mother.

Within a year, however, Nancy's father had found another wife, Sarah Anne Finney, a 45-year-old spinster from Liverpool. Two years later, Sarah Anne gave birth to George's seventh child. It is not known whether Nancy was badly affected by the death of her mother or whether her new stepmother was kind to her, but it is likely that, as the eldest daughter, she had to help look after her younger siblings, including the new baby, her half-sister Alice.

Nancy was also sent out to work at an early age as a child cotton worker in a local mill. It was not until 1910, when aged thirty, that Nancy had married. The 1911 census would find Nancy and her husband, Ramsbottom-born wheelwright William Chadwick, living at 5 Spring Vale, Haslingden. Nancy's nephew, William Barnes, would later confirm to police that Nancy had been widowed since 1921. The Chadwicks had no children and so, following her husband's death, Nancy had needed to continue to work to support herself.

She had served as housekeeper to her landlord, successful stonemason and property owner, John Crabtree, who had lived at 7, Mount Pleasant, Rawtenstall. Whether by chance or by design, Nancy had chosen to work for a wealthy and unmarried octogenarian who had no immediate family. In 1930, her personal fortunes had taken an upward turn when Crabtree died and bequeathed Nancy four of the twelve dwelling houses he owned in the town. His remaining properties, including a row of stone-built terraced cottages named Crabtree Buildings, were shared out between two of his cousins.

Nancy's inheritance comprised four two-bedroom, terraced cottages on Mount Pleasant which, as its name suggests, is in a pleasing elevated location with particularly lovely views. These included number seven, where Crabtree himself had lived, number ten, which Nancy had already been renting from Crabtree for her own occupation, and also numbers nine and twelve. These cottages were of sound construction and still stand.

At the time of her death, Nancy was employed as a live-in housekeeper to another elderly gentleman, which enabled her to rent out all four of her inherited properties. By then, the four houses were commanding a combined weekly rent of one pound seven shillings. Her weekly housekeeper's pay was one pound ten shillings and she was also in receipt of the new state pension, which amounted to one pound six shillings a week. Given that her accommodation and utilities were all found, this total weekly income of four pounds three shillings[2] was more than adequate for a single woman. For comparison, weekly pay for Rawtenstall's police constables at that time was three pounds ten shillings[3].

---

[2] Worth £146.42 at today's values.
[3] £123 at current values.

Nancy's employer at the time of her death was 82-year-old John Edward 'Paddy' Whittaker, a retired railway plate-layer, who rented the house at 81 Hardman Avenue where he and Nancy lived. He was both shocked and saddened when one Det. Chief Inspector McCartney visited him that Sunday afternoon to tell him of Nancy's death, so the policeman kept his questions brief and focused on the issue of Nancy's purse and handbag which had not yet been found.

Whittaker told McCartney that Nancy had visited a nephew at Clough Fold on Sunday 22 August and, on her return, had shown Whittaker a new leather purse which the nephew had given her. Whittaker was able to describe the purse, as he had seen her transferring a pound or two into it before discarding her old purse. He added that Nancy always carried her purse in her bag and always carried her ration book with her, too, as she was *'funny about that'*.

The last time Whittaker had seen his housekeeper was on the Saturday morning, 28 August. He had risen, dressed and gone downstairs at about 8.30 to find her already up and about, with the fire lit. He told McCartney that Nancy had left the house at around 10.30 am, saying *'I'm just going down the street. I'll be back for dinner.'*

In Lancashire, dinner refers to the meal eaten at lunchtime, the evening meal being supper. Whittaker had begun to be concerned, therefore, when Nancy had not returned at lunchtime. His concern had increased when she had not returned for supper, nor indeed at all that night. Doubtless he would have been concerned for himself, too, since he had no food in the house. Whittaker added that he could not recall anyone having called at the house that day. DCI McCartney recorded details of the interview in his notebook but added *'aged witness, recollection not good'*.

Two days later, Whittaker was re-interviewed in greater detail. He told officers he had been widowed around twenty years. Some fifteen years earlier, Nancy had started working for him as a cleaner. He said she had told him her husband had died during the Great War, though the police knew this was not the case.

After inheriting the houses at Mount Pleasant, Nancy had continued to live in one of them initially but, some two or three years ago, had rented out that house also and had moved in with Whittaker to act as his live-in housekeeper. Whittaker explained that he suffered from high blood pressure and that Nancy undertook all his cleaning, washing, ironing and errands.

As is usual, the police asked to see Nancy's room in their search for clues as to her killer. They must have been surprised to be told that Nancy did not have a room of her own, but slept on the couch in the living room. It must have seemed unlikely that a woman in her late sixties had spent every night of the past two or three years sleeping on a couch. Whittaker explained, however, that this was because he had only one bed in the house and very little bedding. If the officers jumped to any unsavoury conclusions regarding Paddy's and Nancy's sleeping arrangements, they did not record these.

Whittaker told them he and Nancy had a bank account at the local savings bank which was for their joint use and in which Nancy would deposit both his savings and her own. This account, he believed, currently held around £27[4]. Whittaker said Nancy had insisted this 'joint' account should be in her name only. He said she would not agree to the account being in both their names and he had gone along with her wishes. Each week, he explained, he gave her some money from his pension to deposit in that supposedly 'joint' account.

Seemingly, the police officers did not question Whittaker's wisdom in having agreed to such a dubious financial arrangement. Since he depended upon Nancy for all his errands, he may have seen no harm in this, especially as he would not have expected Nancy to pre-decease him. Clearly, however, he might now expect to have some difficulty in accessing the funds he held in that account and, indeed, proving that any of that money was his.

Whittaker further said that, every Wednesday, Nancy would go shopping for their joint rations. On Fridays, she would call at the post office to collect his pension. She would collect her own pension on a Tuesday but otherwise had no regular times for going out. Often, she would be accompanied by her good friend, a Mrs Jordan[5]. Nancy often took walks in the evenings, he said, but was usually back between 9 or 9.30 pm, rarely later. He said she did not drink, as she was *'too fond of her money'*.

He added that Nancy personally collected the rents on her four properties fortnightly on a Saturday but, when he had last seen her opening her purse on the day before her death, she had just two or three pounds in it. He described the clothes Nancy had been wearing when she

---

[4] Worth around £943 nowadays.
[5] Mrs Mary Ellen Jordan of 37 Fall Barn Crescent.

had left the house on the Saturday morning as a light-coloured coat and a black, knitted scarf.

The police officer's statement further records Whittaker commenting that, two or three weeks previously, Margaret Allen, the occupant of 137 Bacup Road, had called at his house. Clearly, this comment was not made spontaneously. Given DCI McCartney's earlier observation regarding Whittaker's poor recollection, this comment is likely to have been a response to a specific question posed by the police, who already had their suspicions about Margaret. Naturally enough, they would have wished to establish whether there had been any connection between the deceased and the occupant of the house nearest to where her body was found. However, Whittaker was not asked if there had been any other recent callers to the house.

Whittaker said that, when Margaret Allen had called at his house, she had been dressed like a man and had asked to see Mrs Chadwick. He had not asked what she wanted and nor had he invited her in. He added that she had been up to the house twice in all and he had heard that Nancy had been to Allen's house once, though he did not know why. Speaking of Nancy, Whittaker said *'she's always been very good to me. I shall miss her'*.

The victim's 'abnormality'

In the days following the discovery of Nancy's murder, those locals who had known her – and even some who had not – were volunteering to the press their opinions of her. By all accounts, Nancy was oddly eccentric, extremely miserly and volubly cantankerous. At the brief inquest held in the town the following Wednesday, the only witness to give evidence was Nancy's nephew, 28-year-old William Barnes, the son of Nancy's half-sister Alice Barnes. At the coroner's court, he described Nancy as having been *'abnormal for as long as I have known her'*. Strangely, he then qualified this comment by adding; *'but only in her habits'*.

Barnes, who lived at 2 Ashworth Buildings and worked for the Calico Printers' Association, said his aunt *'always talked sound, with the exception of a couple of occasions'*. He did not elaborate further on this odd remark. He denied his aunt had ever discussed money matters with him, though he said he was aware she owned four houses, and he claimed she had promised to leave him *'a little money'* when she died[6]. This claim, whether true or not, may have been the reason he specified she was only 'abnormal' in her habits, rather than being of unsound mind generally, which might render any bequests subject to legal challenge.

He said his aunt would often call at the houses of strangers and beg a cup of tea. He believed that often she would cadge a meal as well. She would offer to tell fortunes, either from reading the tea leaves or by dealing playing cards. She also went frequently to jumble sales where she would buy odd bits of second hand clothing to wear.

All in all, Barnes painted an unflattering picture of an eccentric and parsimonious scrounger. He said Nancy had called at his house three times during the week before her death but had not found him at home. He was asked if his aunt had had a specific reason for visiting him. He said that she had, although, oddly, he was not asked what that reason was.

Although two women did come forward to say they knew Nancy Chadwick, and one of them described herself as a friend of the deceased, it seems Nancy was not exactly well regarded. Whilst her murder sent ripples of shock around the town, this may have been due to her age and the apparent savagery and sensationalism of the crime, rather than to her popularity.

Her funeral service was conducted by Reverend R.J. Coates, the vicar of St Mary's Evangelical church, and the burial took place at Rawtenstall Cemetery. The press reported that the funeral, which set off from her nephew William's home, was attended by only ten mourners, though at least two of those mourners were in fact policemen. Around twenty curious onlookers observed the burial from outside the cemetery walls.

In comparison to the two hundred townsfolk, mainly women, who would later queue for several hours in the pouring rain to attend Margaret Allen's committal hearing at the town's magistrates' court, those ten mourners and twenty onlookers neither constituted a crowd nor suggested any strength of feeling about the victim. The press would also report that the day of the court hearing, 2nd September, was also Margaret Allen's birthday, but this was another incorrect fact, as Margaret was born on 14 September 1906.

Those same press reports repeated local rumours that Nancy had always distrusted banks and would carry significant amounts of money

---

[6] However, she did not. The sole beneficiary of her will was her younger brother Thomas Barnes, a gas worker.

18

about with her, some of it even being sewn into secret pockets in her clothes. Whilst the money in her 'joint' savings account at the local bank would appear to contradict this impression, and no secret pockets were recorded as having been found in her clothing, the police confirmed that, some years earlier, she had reported being robbed by a young man in the town, during which incident she claimed to have been relieved of £25 in cash[7].

These rumours, and the historic theft, were sufficient to persuade the police to focus on robbery as the most likely motive for Nancy's murder. Whittaker confirmed that, when she had left his house that Saturday morning, Nancy had with her a brown paper carrier bag in which she carried her handbag. He recalled she also owned a black string shopping bag but he did not know whether she had also taken that with her. The absence from the crime scene of Nancy's money and purse, and also her bank and ration books, reinforced the police's suspicions that she had been robbed.

As is usual, doorstep enquiries were made of the neighbouring houses, including that nearest to the spot where the body was found. However, Detective Sergeant John George Thompson may have been unprepared for what he would find when he called at 137 Bacup Road.

---

[7] Worth over £600 at today's values.

Nancy Chadwick – almost cracking a smile – in her 2nd hand jumble sale clothes. (Courtesy of Ron Simpson and Rossendale Civic Trust).

Chapter 3 – The Arrest

'She was extremely irritable and prone to outbursts of anger, and she was agitatedly preoccupied with her own sexual abnormality' – assessment of Margaret Allen, attributed to her friend Annie Cook.[8]

Rumour has it that the first suspect the police pulled in was a night watchman at one of the local mills. He would have been on duty that Saturday evening during the hours Dr Kay believed Nancy had been murdered, and the suspicion was that he had intended to drag the body to the mill's boiler house and dispose of it in the furnace. Given the lack of either motive or any evidence against him, however, the watchman was soon released.

Next, the police would turn their attention to someone else who had no obvious motive. Of all the neighbours to whom the police spoke during their house-to-house enquiries, the one who immediately aroused their suspicion, partly for the proximity of her home to the spot where the body was found but also, perhaps, because of her odd appearance and demeanour, was 41-year-old Miss Margaret Allen. Allen was also known locally as Maggie Allen or Maggie Smith or, more intriguingly, as 'Bill'.

---

[8] Expressed in the words of Huggett and Berry in their book *Daughters of Cain*, Pan Books 1956.

Margaret Allen is arrested
(courtesy of the National Archives)

First impressions

At ten past eight that Sunday morning, when Detective Sergeant Thompson called at her home, this short but stocky former bus conductress was wearing men's pyjamas. She sported a hairstyle known since the 1920s as an 'Eton crop' but which, two decades later, was no longer fashionable. Her slicked-down locks, close-clipped to the nape of the neck, and razor-trimmed sideburns were decidedly mannish.

In 1948, perhaps as a reaction to the bleakness of the war years, British women, even those who worked in factories and mills, were following a trend towards softer, fuller and more feminine hairstyles. In Margaret's case, however, her cultivated deep voice and masculine mannerisms completed an altogether different effect which she deliberately strove to create. If DS Thompson was surprised by her appearance he did not mention this in his notes. Perhaps, though, being a local man, he already knew her by sight.

On entering the house, the Detective Sergeant told Margaret of the body found outside her door and he described the dead woman and the clothes she had been wearing. However, Margaret said she could not help him. In answer to his questions, she said she had neither heard nor seen anything strange during the night, since she had been asleep until he had called. Following this cursory interview, the detective left. For reasons which will become clear later, he may have been over-eager to leave the house.

The house at 137 Bacup Road was as unconventional as its occupant. The dwelling, part single-storey, part double-storey, comprised the right-hand half of an extension to a larger, three-storey building. The larger, original part of the property had been an eighteenth century loom shop, where locals had come to weave wool on communal looms.

Built around 1780 by Richard Ashworth of Cowpe, a wealthy local entrepreneur who also built the nearby Fall Barn Mill for carding and fulling wool, the loom shop had been situated at the north side of the old Haslingden to Todmorden road. Back then, this was little more than an unmade drovers' route and cart track along the riverside.

Whereas, previously, the wool had to be distributed to the weavers to work on in their own cottages around the town, construction of the loom shop meant the weavers could gather in one place to spin the wool and weave it into lengths of cloth using the handlooms provided. The weaving rooms had been arranged on the upper floors which faced south over the Irwell to take advantage of the sunlight which beamed in via triple light windows.

In the 1820s, a new turnpike road[9] was constructed. This road, which would later be designated the Bacup Road or A581, was routed away from the riverside and passed around the other side of the loom shop. Thus, what had been the front of the building, opening onto the old road and the river, now became the back of the premises, and what was formerly the back of the building now fronted the new road.

It is believed to have been around this time that what was now the front of the loom shop was extended to bring the building forward into line with the new road. The extension consisted of a two-storey addition

[9] The turnpike road was built by the legendary 'Blind Jack of Knaresborough'.

with a narrow, single-storey section in front of that. The single-storey part of the extension served firstly as a toll-keeper's booth. It had stone walls, some of which were over a foot thick, with arrow-slit windows via which the toll-keeper might listen out for approaching traffic then slip out to collect the toll fares. It is likely that the toll-keeper and his family lived in the two-storey part of the extension. Over the doorway to the toll-house was an elaborate stone escutcheon bearing the arms of the entrepreneurial Ashworth family who owned the land around and were trustees of the turnpike.

The old loom shop (now *The Weaver's Cottage*), on the other side of which 137 Bacup Road was attached. (With kind permission of Rossendale Civic Trust)

The advent of large steam-powered looms marked the demise of manually operated looms such as those used in the loom shop, and, later still, the supplies of raw cotton arriving from America via Liverpool saw the town's woollen mills converted to cotton production. In 1881, the county's turnpike roads were taken over by the local authorities and so the system of paying tolls was abandoned. The redundant toll-keeper's booth attached to the old loom shop was next brought into use as a lock-up for drunks and petty criminals. It was used for this purpose for a decade or so until the town's police station was built in the 1890s.

Sometime thereafter, it is not known exactly when, the loom shop and its extensions became residential accommodation. The extended, single- and two-storey half of the building, which faced the Bacup Road, was divided into two small and very basic dwellings. The single-storey sections were further divided and utilised as coal stores and small sculleries (they could not properly be called kitchens). Each scullery had a shallow stone sink and cold-water tap, used for all the occupants' ablutions. Only the arrow-slit windows, one of which was by then extended and glazed, gave a clue as to the extension's earlier functions. It was the right-hand one of those two properties which Margaret Allen would rent from Greenbank Estates Ltd., the company which had taken over management of the Ashworths' estates.

There was no bathroom or toilet in Margaret's house, though this was true of many working-class houses in Rawtenstall and in other industrial towns, well into the second half of the twentieth century. The nearest toilet facilities were in a communal block situated in the ginnel or alley alongside the former loom shop, and they served it and the surrounding cottages. The numerous families who shared this facility would take turns at cleaning the toilets.

Entering Margaret's home, DS Thompson found the scullery immediately to the left and the door to the coal store immediately to the right. Another door just a couple of feet beyond the front door led into the double-storey part of the house. This comprised, on the ground floor, a living room measuring around eighteen feet by sixteen feet, with a fireplace and a stone staircase leading to the single upstairs bedroom. There was only one entrance to the house and that was the front door.

The front door of the adjoining dwelling, to the left of Margaret's house, was located to the side of the building, around the corner in Fall Barn Close. Margaret's living room had two small side windows which looked out onto the side alley, and another small window, which was set into the front wall but extended from a point some six feet above the floor. That window afforded some light but no view out. During Margaret's occupation of these very basic premises, the Ashworth's stone escutcheon still sat in place, proudly if incongruously.

Although those two front dwellings would be demolished around 1972 during the town's improvement schemes, the older portion of the building, that which had been the three-storey loom shop, was retained

25

and these days serves as the town's heritage centre. Known locally as *The Weavers' Cottage*, it is maintained and run by volunteers of the Rossendale Civic Trust and is a very popular local attraction.

137 Bacup Road during the 1972 demolition. The single-storey section of Margaret's house is to the right and extends from the white-capped window, past the front door and the now exposed coal place. This entire side of the building, from the second chimney on the left forward, would be demolished, leaving just the older, original section of the building standing. (Rossendale Civic Trust).

Visitors come from far and wide to see this remarkable asset and to observe demonstrations of weaving on the centre's original handlooms. The demolished section of the building, comprising the plot formerly occupied by Margaret's house and its adjacent dwelling, is now paved over, with nothing to indicate the tragedy which occurred here in 1948.

During Margaret Allen's occupation, number 137 was in very poor condition. Inside, the property was very sparsely furnished and was also extremely dirty. The only good thing which could be said of the property was that, from the front bedroom window, it had a good outlook. Situated opposite the local cricket ground, the bedroom of the property enjoyed a good view of the hills. If he formed any impressions of either the house or its occupant, however, DS Thompson did not make a note of these.

The ginnel and communal toilets alongside 137 Bacup Rd.
(Courtesy of Steve Yates and Rossendale Civic Trust)

Linking victim and suspect

The Irwell ran behind 137 Bacup Road, some eighty odd yards away. Leading over the river at this point was Fall Barn Crossing – a railway bridge and pedestrian crossing – beneath which was a weir. This seemed like a good potential dumping spot for the victim's missing bag and for the murder weapon, neither of which had been found near the body.

Accordingly, that Sunday afternoon, policemen conducted a search of the river bank, whilst several sappers, volunteers from the local army camp, waded thigh-deep in the water of the weir. Press reports described in detail how the men poked about with sticks in the silt of the river bed, whilst a police bloodhound sniffed around in the undergrowth along the banks. The pressmen reported that the bloodhound was named 'Lubin'. This probably reflects the fact that, at this stage, the pressmen had little other detail to fill their columns.

Meanwhile, a small and curious crowd of locals, Margaret Allen amongst them, stood watching the search. Detectives also stood by, though they were busy observing the reactions of the crowd. Suddenly, the voice of a woman onlooker called out: *'There's a bag in the water! Look, it's down there!'*

Those same pressmen would later assert – damningly but wrongly – that the onlooker who spotted the bag was Margaret Allen herself. One of the policemen duly retrieved from the water a string shopping bag, inside which was a brown, imitation leather handbag. This would later be confirmed as belonging to the victim. Inside the bag, were sewing materials, including three pairs of scissors, and some playing cards, but no purse or cash. A matching playing card was found lying nearby on the river bank, suggesting the bag had been dumped in the river at this location, not further upstream.

Before television ownership became widespread, many people tuned in to their radios, the signal for which was piped into their houses via a local radio relay system. Additionally, they visited their local cinemas once or twice a week for entertainment. It was for this reason that the Scotland Yard detectives suggested these media be used to message the local populace requesting information about Nancy Chadwick. They were keen to hear from anyone who had seen Nancy on the day she was killed.

CID officers also widened the radius of the search area, visiting homes, not only in the vicinity of the crime scene, but also in the streets around Hardman Avenue, where the deceased had lived, and numerous statements were taken.

Margaret speaks
On Tuesday 31 August, Margaret Allen called in at the Rawtenstall Police Station on North Street to make a statement. Whether she was summoned there, either routinely or specifically, or whether she simply went on her own initiative, is not recorded. Though, seemingly, she had been unable to recognise the victim from the description given two days earlier by Det. Sgt Thompson, she now confirmed she had

28

known Nancy Chadwick, albeit very slightly. Detective Superintendent John Woodmansey conducted her interview and this is the statement she gave:

'I went to my present address in 1942 where I live alone. There are two rooms and I pay six shillings and fourpence a week rent.[10] I shall be forty-two years of age on 2 September 1948[11]. I have known Mrs Chadwick for about three weeks to one month. I was in Mrs Haworth's house at 13A Longholme Road about one month ago when an old lady came in for a pint of tea – Mrs Chadwick. I met her again a week later and she said she was looking for sugar. I said if I had some spare I'd bring it to her house. I haven't done any work since January 1948. I live on eleven shillings[12] a week from public assistance and get twenty-six shillings[13] a week from the National Health sick. I often borrow money.'

Like Paddy Whittaker's statement, this does not read as a spontaneous account, but rather as answers to specific questions put to someone who was, quite obviously, a suspect.

Fall Barn Weir, where Nancy's bag was found. (Author's photo)

---

[10] This would be worth £11.06 at today's values.
[11] Actually, her birthday was 14th September. Owing to what we will see was an erratic childhood, she may not have known her exact date of birth.
[12] Worth £19.21 today.
[13] Worth £45.41 today.

The home search

Following this interview, Chief Superintendent Woodmansey and Chief Inspector Stevens escorted Allen back to her home where a search of the premises was conducted. They recorded that the house consisted of one upstairs bedroom, a single downstairs living room, leading off which, and situated on the left immediately by the front door, was a very small scullery.

Scotland Yard man Stevens noted that the fire range looked particularly clean (perhaps in comparison with the rest of the premises) and he asked Margaret whether she had cleaned it recently, but she denied that she had. Clearly, Stevens was mindful of the traces of ashes found on Nancy Chadwick's body.

Upstairs in the bedroom, an armchair was pushed up against another fireplace which was blocked off with a sheet of metal. However, Woodmansey formed the opinion that the fireplace had been like this for *'a long time'*. The police search seems to have been a rather cursory one, as nothing unusual, significant or incriminating was found. Like Detective Sergeant Thompson, Woodmansey and Stevens did not linger long in Margaret's house. For reasons not recorded, however, the two detectives decided to visit the premises a second time, at noon the following day, Wednesday 1st September.

On their second visit, they now noticed, to the right just inside the front door, another door which led to the coalhouse. It seems remarkable that they had failed either to notice or to examine the coalhouse on their first visit. They also noticed something else they had missed earlier, but which was clearly of crucial importance. Just inside the front door, low down on the wall to the right of the coalhouse door, were what Woodmansey now suspected might be three sizeable bloodstains. Asked for an explanation of the marks, Margaret made no reply.

Back in the living room, Woodmansey spotted yet another thing he had had not noticed on the previous day – a shopping bag on the floor at the far side of the room. It contained ashes and three pieces of rag. Margaret said the contents had come from the upstairs grate and had been there around three weeks. Woodmansey must have been doubtful about this statement, since he had already decided the upstairs fireplace had been boarded up for a long time. On closer inspection, he found that two of the rags in the bag were dry but the third was damp and *'maroon-coloured'*.

Curiosity prompted him to ask Margaret what she had used the rags for. She replied that they were floor cloths. Then, to his great surprise, she suddenly walked over to the sofa, picked up her mackintosh which was lying there and said, *'come on. I'll tell you all about it.'* Margaret was cautioned by Stevens at this stage and she simply said, *'let's get out of here.'* As the three headed for the front door, Margaret pointed to the coalhouse and said, coolly, *'that's where I put her.'* The detectives must have been surprised yet elated to have not only identified the killer but to have also obtained a confession only five days into the murder enquiry. Margaret was duly arrested and taken to Rawtenstall's North Street police station.

The confession

On arrival at the police station, Margaret said she now wished to tell the truth. She was duly booked in as a prisoner and was searched by Policewoman Marjorie Dodds. Dodds recorded that Margaret had on her just one shilling, one penny, two halfpennies and two farthings.[14] This cash and some of her clothing, shoes and effects taken from her home were retained as evidence by the police.

With the detectives' help, Margaret made another written statement after which she was charged that she had, on or around 28 August, murdered Mrs Nancy Chadwick, to which charge she replied *'I did.'* Although she was again cautioned that she was not obliged to say anything unless she wished to do so, but that whatever she did say would be taken down in writing and might be given in evidence, Margaret made it known that she did wish to say something. In fact, she had quite a lot to say. She gave the following statement freely under caution:

'The other statements I have told you are wrong. I was coming out of the house on Saturday morning about 9.20 and Mrs Chadwick came around the corner. She asked if this was where I lived and could she come in.

I told her I was going out. I was in a funny mood and she just seemed to get on my nerves, though she hadn't said anything. I told her to go as I was going out and she could come another time but she seemed to insist on coming in.

---

[14] Worth about £3.78 at today's values.

I just happened to look around and saw a hammer in the kitchen. By this time, we were talking just inside the kitchen with the front door shut. On the spur of the moment, I hit her with the hammer. She gave a shout that seemed to start me off more. I hit her a few times. But I don't know how many. I pulled the body in my coal house. It was there all day.

I have told you where I was all day. That part was true and I went to bed about ten to eleven o'clock. I slept, I don't know how long. When I awoke the thought of what was downstairs kept me awake. I went downstairs. I don't know the time as all the clocks are broken. There were no lights in the road and I couldn't hear footsteps. My intention was to try and pull her to the river and dispose of the body but it was too heavy, so I just put it on the road.

I went back to bed and didn't get up again till the officer came to the door. I heard the noise and knew they had found the body. I looked out the window and saw the bus. I went back to bed and fell asleep.

Just before I put the body out, I went round the corner and threw the bag in the river. Also the hammer head I hit her with. I threw them some distance up the river. The handle I used for the fire. I looked in the bag but there was no money. I didn't actually kill her for that. I had one of my funny moods.

The bag you found this morning has the ashes from the floor of the coal house. They were there when I put the body in there, and the antimacassar I burned on the Sunday.[15] I had no reason at all. It seemed to come over me. After she shouted, after the first hit, that seemed to set me off.'

---

[15] Mr Whittaker would later advise that what Nancy usually wore as a headscarf was in fact a black antimacassar – a knitted cloth covering for the backs of sofas and armchairs, intended to protect them from commonly worn hair dressing products such as Macassar oil.

Fall Barn Crossing, as it was in 1940s. The Irwell, culverted at this point, runs alongside the railway line (now gone), passing beneath the pedestrian bridge and the signal box. The weir (not visible) is nearby. The loom shop, with its distinctive triple windows, is in the distance. The cottages situated in front of it are all now demolished. Margaret's house (not visible) is situated on the other side of the loom shop fronting onto the Bacup Road. The crenelated structure on the right is Albion Mill, now replaced by a modern health centre. (Source unattributable).

137 Bacup Road, partly demolished, reveals the lobby between the front door and the living room door. A darkened section of wall delineates the coal place, where the body of Nancy Chadwick was kept. The Scullery is to the left of the front door. (Rossendale Civic Trust).

A close-up view of the tiny and confined lobby and scullery, where a fatal altercation took place on 28 August 1948. (Rossendale Civic Trust).

Chapter 4 – The Accused

'She had a particular reputation for kindness to the old and infirm,' –
General Manager Rawtenstall Corporation Motor Transport Department.

Press reports, often informed by tip-offs from the police themselves, described Margaret Allen as being 'a well-known figure' around Rawtenstall as well as in nearby Bacup. She was distinctive because of her masculine appearance and also because she insisted people should call her 'Bill'. Indeed, she refused to answer to 'Margaret'. It was suggested that, albeit in her own way, she was as eccentric and 'abnormal' as the murder victim Nancy Chadwick.

Margaret's background
An interim police report, undated and unsigned and written on or after 2 September 1948, reads as follows:

'Margaret Allen – identity card number NTMQ-82-2 – aged 42 – no previous convictions registered at this office.[16] She is represented by Kenneth Yates of the firm Robert Arthur Cotton, 1 Dale Street, Haslingden. The Accused's rented house (rent is six shillings and fourpence a week) is absolutely filthy. The front door opens onto the

---

[16] This would turn out not to be the case.

pavement and leads to a small scullery containing a sink. Immediately to the right of the front door is a step leading to the only room on the ground floor. This is sparsely furnished and has two doors leading to cupboards. Another door leads to an upstairs bedroom which only contained a bed and an armchair, pushed up against the fire grate.

The house is in the main road, and the junction road, Fall Barn Fold, leads to a railway level crossing some eighty yards distant. Running parallel with the railway is the river and over the crossing and up the hill is Hardman Avenue. It is about half a mile from this house[17] to the Bacup road.'

A police officer in the case (believed to be one Jock Tulloch) subsequently conducted enquiries into Margaret's background and antecedents and seems to have done a remarkably thorough job. His highly comprehensive, though unsigned report, dated 27 October 1948, records Margaret's history from childhood.

The report states that Margaret Allen, a single woman, was born in Bolton on 14 September 1906[18]. She was the illegitimate daughter of Alice Dobson (née Parkinson, alias Smith, alias Allen) and John Joseph Lycett (alias Smith, alias Allen). Dobson and Lycett had lived together on and off as a couple but never married. Although Margaret's parents were named on her birth record as Alice Allen, formerly Dobson, and John Joseph Lycett, research reveals there is, indeed, no marriage record for the couple.

Margaret's father was born on 5 November 1851 in Ireland and was a journeyman[19] boot and shoe maker. The report states that, prior to his association with Alice Dobson, Lycett had been living in Bolton with his lawful wife Jane Lycett (née Moss) and their three children, but Lycett had left his wife around 1898 to co-habit with Alice, and police believed that Lycett's children from his marriage were all deceased prior to 1948.

Margaret's mother had been born Alice Parkinson in 1865. Records show that, in 1885 when aged twenty, she had married one Thomas Dobson, but he had died less than four years later. Despite the brevity of Alice's marriage, the police report states that, in 1898 when she had first taken up with John Lycett, she was a 33-year-old widow and

---

[17] That is, the victim's house on Hardman Avenue.

[18] At 4 Blundell St., according to her birth certificate.

[19] 'Journeyman' means a casual employee, paid by the day, not in fixed employment.

mother of sixteen children. If this is true, Alice must have given birth to one child each year since the age of seventeen. None of those sixteen children was living with her in 1898, as they were all either deceased or in the care of the parish or the poorhouse.

Given the short duration of her marriage, most of those sixteen children must have been born out of wedlock. Six further children were born of the later association between Alice Dobson and John Lycett. Only four of them, Margaret included, were still living by 1948. Thus, remarkable though it seems, Margaret was the twentieth of twenty-two children born to her mother.

The police report states that Lycett was addicted to drink and, from time to time, would leave Alice to travel around the country. He would also change his name whenever he went roaming. His reasons for doing so were not explored by the police, who stated he was not believed to have a criminal record. However, research reveals a John Lycett does feature in Preston court records in the 1870s, using the alias George Williamson when arrested and imprisoned for several offences of larceny. The record has insufficient detail to link it with Margaret Allen's father, though it seems he was inclined to use aliases.

According to the police officer drafting the 1948 report, whenever a child was born of their association Alice Dobson would register it in whichever surname Lycett was using at the time, and the children would also undergo a further change of surname from time to time. This explains why Margaret Allen was better known by some around Rawtenstall as Maggie Smith.

In 1908, the report adds, Lycett had left home, leaving Dobson and four of their children without any means of support. Of necessity, two of the four surviving children still in Alice's care – Mary Alice and Maria – were sent to Leyfield School, a 'poor house' in West Derby, Liverpool. The younger two, John and Margaret (she was then 2 years old), were sent to Wavertree Cottages, Liverpool.[20] Some two years later, the family were reunited with Lycett and living together at Holmes Buildings, Bacup.

Between August and September 1919, however, as Margaret reaches her thirteenth birthday, Lycett is recorded as being an in-patient at Rawtenstall's Moorland Institution (a workhouse, formerly known as the Haslingden Union). He is using the name of John Joseph Smith and

---

[20] Wavertree Cottage Homes comprised sixteen cottages and was a 'home for pauper children' below eight years of age.

tells the workhouse keeper he has no next of kin, but gives Alice Dobson's name as 'a friend'. On 23 May 1927, the report continues, 75-year-old Lycett died, at the Moorland Institution, of bronchitis and heart failure. Having been widowed for more than fifteen years, Margaret's mother Alice died on 25 January 1943, the cause of her death being given simply as 'old age'.

When the reporting officer's enquiries later took him to Bacup to interview Margaret's older sister, Mary Alice Peel, she would confirm that their parents had never married. She told him Lycett had been a good man when sober but was addicted to drink and, when under its influence, would be violent towards Alice. Peel would recall incidents from her childhood when Lycett had struck their mother with a rolling pin or a poker. These incidents had gone unreported to the police, as indeed the majority of incidents of domestic violence did back then. Since most women were wholly, or at least mainly dependent for support upon their men folk, any period the wage-earner spent in prison would mean their dependents facing destitution.

Bacup days

Although born in Bolton, Margaret had spent her early childhood (apart from the two years in the children's home) in Plantation Street, Bacup. The houses here were severely overcrowded, four-storey tenements, the lower two storeys of which were built against an earth bank, whilst the top two storeys were above ground. These houses had been demolished by the 1930s and replaced by back-to-back terraces which still stand.

In Margaret's childhood, Plantation Street was also known locally as 'Irish Bank' owing to the fact that the street's residents were mainly Irish. Like the other local children, Margaret would play on the steep, grassy banks which rose up behind the town's shops and houses, in a spot known locally as 'the Bonks'. Beyond the town lay the moors, a place of wild beauty to which the townsfolk might escape on Sundays and holidays.

Margaret had attended St Saviour Church of England School in Bacup to begin with, and later St Mary's Roman Catholic School at Haslingden until aged 14. In 1913, Margaret had her first holy communion administered by Father Keily at St Mary's Catholic Church in Haslingden, but she never got around to being confirmed in the

Catholic religion. Margaret's childhood, however, was a lamentably short one by today's standards.

From the age of twelve, she had begun work as a half-timer cotton operative at Springholme Mill, Bacup, and attended school on a part-time basis, too. It was quite common, well into the 20th century, for children to work a gruelling half day in the mills and to attend school for the remaining half. John Robert Clynes, a Lancashire MP and former child millworker, who served as Home Secretary from 1929 to 1931, had campaigned vigorously for improvements in working conditions for child labourers in the cotton industry.

Bacup from an old postcard. (Author's collection).

Margaret in uniform

The police report lists a number of different cotton mills around Bacup at which Margaret Allen subsequently worked. What the report does not include, however, is Margaret's voluntary wartime service, which gives more of a flavour of her character.

In 1939, many local men who were either above or below the qualifying age range to sign up, joined the Local Defence Volunteers or, as it later became known, the Home Guard. In 1941, during a period of great tension, when it was feared a German invasion was imminent, rules were changed to also allow women to join the Home Guard. Indeed, half of the volunteers in the Bacup unit of the 31st Battalion Rossendale and Rawtenstall Home Guard were women. Like the men, the women of the Home Guard were ready to fight to the death in the event of invasion. One of the first women in Bacup to join the Home Guard was Margaret Allen.

Initially, the women were issued with feminine hats and mackintoshes, modelled on the uniform worn by the Women's Royal Voluntary Service of the day. Those Home Guard women who wished, however, could have the full khaki battle dress, complete with boots and forage cap, which was more practical apparel for when they were crawling through undergrowth, practising self-defence techniques or undertaking weapons and explosives training.

Margaret was so proud of her khaki combats, and perhaps so much at ease in such masculine attire, that she had herself photographed wearing it. This (see page 43) is one of the few photographs of Margaret which exist.

The police report records that, initially, Margaret's paid wartime employment from 31st January 1941 till 9th July 1942 was one which also supplied a uniform. She worked as a temporary post woman at GPO Bacup. Suspended on 25th June 1942, however, when accused of the theft of a registered letter, she subsequently resigned. No further action seems to have been taken with regard to the alleged theft.

From Home Guard to bus guard

Nine days later, Margaret put on yet another uniform when she began work as a wartime bus conductress, also termed a bus guard or 'clippie'. The indications are that she greatly enjoyed this work and, moreover, was well regarded by the bus company and bus passengers alike.

Indeed, in 1955, the General Manager of Rawtenstall Corporation Motor Transport would tell Huggett and Berry – somewhat ironically, in view of her conviction – that *'she had a particular reputation for kindness to the old and infirm'*, and he said her record would be *'a credit to anyone'*. This firmly contradicts some of the more scurrilous 1948 press reports which suggested she was fired for verbally abusing and even physically assaulting passengers.

Moreover, several local residents, who were children back then, can recall to this day Margaret's kindness in distributing her limited sweet ration amongst the local youngsters. In 1955, Huggett and Berry would encounter one local chap who assured them that Margaret was one of the kindest of the bus conductors, even when wartime petrol shortages meant bus services were reduced and overcrowding was the usual state of affairs.

'Reet civil the lass was,' he told them, *'no matter how full she was, that lass never put you off the bus.'* Another local resident, who was a child at the time, recalls in particular Margaret's kindness to mothers travelling with small children and prams. She would never see someone struggling with parcels or babies but would rush to help them board the bus.

In the police report, it is suggested that, when Margaret left her job on the buses four years later on 29 June 1946, it was owing to ill-health, and this fact, too, was widely reported in the press. However, this seems most unlikely to have been the case. Like all the other women employed on the buses, Margaret had been engaged as a *temporary* conductress for the duration of the war. Just as they had done during The Great War, women had stepped up once again in 1939 to fill many occupations hitherto held exclusively by men. In this respect, the war had provided a woman of Margaret's masculine inclinations with a desirable opportunity to undertake a man's job.

Rawtenstall Bus and Tram Shed where Margaret was based. (Source unattributable).

Margaret Allen in Home Guard days. (Source unattributable).

In June 1945, however, with the ending of hostilities in Europe, the demobilisation of 4.3 million servicemen had begun. Even with victory assured in the Far East also, this slow process would continue until December 1947. As the servicemen gradually returned from overseas, some of them from Japanese internment camps, the women who had been filling their jobs were arbitrarily dismissed. The end of June 1946 saw most bus conductresses [including the author's mother] ousted from their jobs.

Dismissal was a bitter blow to those women who had enjoyed the skills and the financial independence the work had given them. This was especially so for unmarried women like Margaret Allen, who had no other source of income and who now had to compete with the demobilised men for work. Redundancy is, therefore, a much more likely reason for Margaret having quit a job which she clearly enjoyed.

Margaret works as a labourer
Another indicator that ill-health is unlikely to have been the reason Margaret left her bus conductress job on 29 June was that, just two days later, on 1st July 1946, she began work as a full-time chromium plater's labourer with the Middlesex Gun Company at Rawtenstall's Hall Carr Mill. It makes no sense to suggest she was so ill she had to quit a job she loved, yet immediately took on an even more physically demanding job. Even had she left voluntarily, perhaps attracted by higher wages or the appeal of a manly labouring job, she would not have needed to provide a false excuse to the bus company which was already laying off the female workforce. Any resignation would have been gratefully accepted.

Margaret must also have known that the armaments companies were running down production and that Hall Carr Mill would very soon resume textile manufacturing, reducing opportunities both for men's labouring work and for the lucrative overtime working of the war years. It seems more likely, therefore, that, like all the conductresses, she was made redundant and had no choice but to seek work at a mill.

Dishonesty and dismissal
Margaret was indeed soon engaged in women's work again when Hall Carr Mill reverted to textile production, and she remained there for just over a year. Unfortunately, she was then discharged for theft.

44

Records show she stole, from a fellow employee, a note book and savings stamps to the value of thirty-five shillings.[21] On 7 August 1947, she was convicted of larceny in connection with that theft and was fined forty shillings.[22]

Later that month, she secured a woman's job as a stitcher at Hirst's slipper factory, but left some five months later in January 1948. Ill-health is again cited as the cause but, this time, her GP's confirmation of her illness meant she now began to receive the newly introduced sickness benefit. This illness must have been debilitating indeed, for, despite the fact that her work had been a useful means by which she had been able to define herself as a man, Margaret would never work again.

Also on the police file, is a crime report dated 15 May 1947 [reference CRO P5645] containing details of a break-in which had occurred on 12 May at the Rawtenstall premises of Messrs Dubarry Modes of London. During the burglary, dresses, cash and sewing machines to the value of £684.12s[23] were stolen.

Margaret Allen does not appear to have been charged with or convicted of that offence, so it is unclear why the report is on her file. This was not the type of petty and opportunistic theft to which she had been tempted previously, but was one which would have required an accomplice, transport, storage and a contact willing to 'fence' the stolen items.

This crime report may have been mis-filed or, this being a time when the police had little compunction about 'fitting up' a suspect, it may be that the police were hoping to boost their clear-up rate by pinning another offence on a suspect whom they already had in custody. This is a seemingly insignificant point, but it may give us a sense of how the police operated back then.

Whilst it seems odd that that this should have been included in the police file, what is odder still is what was *not* included. Strangely, what the police did not address in their interviewing of Margaret Allen was her fairly obvious 'gender dysphoria'.

---

[21] Worth around £61 at today's values.

[22] Worth about £70 today.

[23] Worth over £25,000 at today's values.

Chapter 5 – The Elephant in the Room

'She denies absolutely any homosexual or other abnormal tendencies' –
G.A.H. Cormack, Medical Officer, HM Prison Strangeways.

If Margaret's strange habit of wearing men's clothes and insisting she be addressed as 'Bill' were one of the reasons the police thought it worth bringing her in for interview, this does not factor in their reports. Her men's clothing and mannish mannerisms were not addressed by them at this stage. It is just possible the police did not wish to be accused of any sort of prejudice. Alternatively, it may be that they realised Margaret's peculiarities would be obvious to a judge and jury who might then make up their own minds as to what, if any, relevance it had to her motive in killing Nancy.

More likely, perhaps, the policemen did not understand her gender anomaly and may not have been able to put it into words. They may have wanted to keep the case simple and straightforward. Like Margaret herself, the police would not have had access to the appropriate terminology to describe her disposition. The terms 'transgender' and 'transsexual' were only introduced in 1949, after Margaret's death, and would not appear in popular usage until the 1960s. If, like Huggett and Berry, they thought her a lesbian, they may have felt this was simply a perversion of habit. They may have considered this an avenue they did not wish to explore and one not relevant to the case in hand, which was, in their opinion, a straightforward case of murder in the course of a robbery.

Margaret Allen's GP, John Ashton Lees, of Bank House, Rawtenstall, also provided a statement to police:

'I know Margaret Allen, my patient under the National Health Insurance, since 1944. Since 30 May 1944 up to 2 September 1944 I saw her at home and at my surgery on twenty-one occasions, suffering from dyspepsia and cystitis.

In February 1945 on one occasion medicine for vertigo; August 1945 once for a burn on the hand; 22 August 1945 to 13 September five visits for vertigo.

1946, I saw her on twenty-one occasions – general debility, anaemia and on one occasion she said she had had a fainting attack. 1947 – I attended her three times: March – conjunctivitis; September – respiratory catarrh, November – she had a black eye and complained she had been assaulted by someone the previous day.

January 1948 – she commenced visiting the surgery complaining of feeling sickly, a dyspeptic attack; January to 26 May 1948 – seen by me twenty-one times, treated for dyspepsia; February – complained of pain in her left side. Arranged for her to see Surgeon Dr Taylor at Bury Infirmary: "slight degree of hydro nephrosis in right kidney; some calcified glands present in urinary tract".

He arranged for her to be admitted. 28 May 1948, examined under anaesthetic – uterus was small but nothing abnormal found. Discharged 10 June 1948. Since then she had visited my surgery weekly, generally to get a certificate of inability to follow employment. Not seriously ill in any way but suffering anaemia and general debility.'

By anyone's standards, twenty-one visits to one's GP in a three-month period, and subsequently forty-two visits in two years, is greatly excessive. Nowadays, one hopes this would arouse sufficient concern for a GP to consider exploring the reasons behind such frequent and diverse illnesses.

According to NHS information literature, 'Dyspepsia' covers a group of digestive symptoms, including heartburn, involuntary regurgitation of food or liquids, loss of appetite, pain, discomfort or bloating, and common causes of dyspepsia include anxiety and depression.

Whilst Margaret's troubles with her waterworks may have been due to her poor personal hygiene and self-neglect, of which we shall hear more later, her vertigo, vomiting, claimed historic fainting fits and abdominal pains fall within a range of 'invisible' complaints, all of which, according to NHS literature, might also have been rooted in anxiety or depression.

The distress these bouts caused may have been apparent enough to Dr Lees, however, as he never suggests he suspected Margaret of malingering, but he continued to sign her weekly certificates enabling her to qualify for sickness payments and public assistance. Oddly, despite the possible emotional causes for her reported maladies, there is no comment in his statement regarding the state of Margaret's mental health.

The gender issue

Like the police, Dr Lees makes no mention of what medical practitioners of the day would term her 'gender dysphoria' or 'gender confusion'. It may be that, like many others before and since, including Huggett and Berry, he believed Margaret was a lesbian and he did not wish to address the private matter of her sexual proclivities. Perhaps he saw no connection between her sexual orientation and her physical or mental health. What we know nowadays about the prejudicial treatment and consequent emotional turmoil of transgendered individuals was not widely known or considered in 1948, not even by the bulk of the medical profession.

The police officer who conducted the background checks on Margaret does not appear to have checked for any report connected with the alleged assault which had led to Margaret's black eye, or to have queried the circumstances in which she received this injury. No criminal case seems to have resulted from this incident either, so perhaps Margaret did not report it to the police at the time. Of course, she may have given her assailant as good as she got. Whether this assault was prompted by Margaret's unconventional appearance, and whether she felt too embarrassed to report it, is, like many other unexplored aspects of the case, a matter for conjecture. If there were other such assaults upon her over the years, Margaret did not report them, either to the police or to her GP.

However, the police officer did enquire into her earlier health records which pre-dated those of Dr Lees. These, too, revealed a growing frequency of diverse medical problems. In 1924, Margaret had been treated for a suppurating finger and, in March 1930, for a crushed thumb, which, presumably, were straightforward industrial accidents. No sickness was recorded in the six years between these events. Indeed, she seems to have been in reasonably good health up until 1930. Her history of frequent medical complaints seems to date from that year.

From April to June 1930, 23-year-old Margaret was treated for diphtheria (a highly contagious and potentially fatal bacterial infection, for which routine vaccination would not be introduced until 1940). Thereafter, she was treated for a series of coughs, bouts of colic, arthritis, bronchitis and tonsillitis. Respiratory ailments and infections were known to be common amongst textile workers, so some of these could also have been work-related.

Five years later, however, on 29 August 1935, Margaret underwent surgery at St Mary's gynaecological hospital in Manchester for dysmenorrhoea (painful menstrual cramps). This procedure may have been particularly invasive or may have had significant after effects, because she remained at that hospital for three months as an in-patient. This seems an excessive length of stay, especially as she was then living with her mother and, if discharged sooner, might have been cared for at home. If there were any complications arising from this surgery, or if any other kinds of treatment were administered during her stay in hospital, this is not noted in her GP's records.

Was Margaret a man?

According to Huggett and Berry's enquiries, it was following her release from St Mary's that she began telling people she had in fact undergone a sex-change operation and was now, physically, a man. They believed it was from this time also that she began to insist on being called 'Bill' and would no longer answer to 'Margaret'.

Gender re-assignment surgery was not generally available in 1935, however, and even had it been, it would have been expensive and well beyond Margaret's means. There is no doubt, therefore, that Margaret's claim to have undergone such a procedure was merely wishful thinking on her part. Moreover, a later surgeon's report of 1948 remarks upon the small size of Margaret's uterus. The surgeon does not seem to have drawn any particular conclusion from this, such as a possible imbalance of hormones, but he would surely have mentioned the *absence* of a uterus or the removal or re-fashioning of any external genital organs, had any sex change surgery really taken place.

49

In 1936, having again complained of abdominal pains, Margaret spent a further month back at St Mary's being treated for suspected pelvic peritonitis [a common cause of which, in women, is inflammation of the fallopian tubes]. This, too, would suggest Margaret was, physically at least, female. Further exploratory surgery was carried out on that occasion and the surgeon's conclusion was 'no gynaecological abnormality detected'. Following this treatment, she was transferred to the large and gothic Barnes Convalescent Hospital in Cheadle, Cheshire, to recuperate.

In 1948, after Margaret's arrest, she was remanded to Strangeways prison where she came under the care of the Prison Medical Officer, George Arthur Hay Cormack. He interviewed Margaret and, unlike Dr Lees, decided to address the issue of her sexuality. He established that she had remained single and had lived with her mother until the latter's death in 1943, since which time she had lived alone. Cormack states: *'the home conditions are described as very poor'* and adds:

> *'It has been her custom for the past several years to wear trousers and pullover. She explains she acquired this type of attire when employed as a bus conductress, found it convenient and continued the practice. She denies absolutely any homosexual or other abnormal tendencies. She explains she remained a spinster as it was necessary for her to care for her mother and this was not compatible with marriage. She frankly admits occasional normal sexual intercourse.'*

Of course, there is no way of establishing the truth of her assertion that she had experienced occasional 'normal' intercourse (in Cormack's book, presumably, this would be heterosexual). Surely, though, what would have been a pertinent next question would have been one about relationships? Cormack does not query with whom this 'spinster' might have had occasional intercourse or, indeed, whether or not it had been consensual.

Like Dr Lees, he does not question the circumstances in which she received a black eye, even though he is trying to assess her mental state and determine whether that mental state could have caused her to kill someone. Was Margaret a natural aggressor, or was she a victim of aggressive bullying by others? Surely, these would have been relevant issues and ones which he ought to have explored? Yet he did not.

50

It is interesting to speculate on why, having spent the previous thirteen years insisting she was a man and demanding to be addressed as 'Bill', Margaret now tells the prison doctor that her cross-dressing was simply a matter of convenience. Despite the fact that she was still wearing men's attire, and although the police search of her home turned up no female clothing, Margaret seems to have been unwilling to open up about her conviction that she was essentially male. Perhaps she felt intimidated in the prison environment, or maybe she felt inhibited about discussing such an intimate issue with a stranger. As later events will show, however, she may have had an altogether different reason for avoiding questions about her gender and sexuality.

The prison MO's inquisition was to continue along intrusive lines. Cormack further questioned Margaret about her menstruation and she told him this had been most erratic but had now almost ceased. She also described periodic bouts of dizziness followed by irritability, during which the least thing would annoy her and said she would, at times, kick or throw items of furniture about the home. Cormack seems to have accepted this was normal menopausal behaviour.

Mental health issues?

Cormack reviewed the police and GP's reports and, from these and his interviews with Margaret, he determined there had been no family history of mental illness. Surprisingly, he does not appear to have consulted the medical records of other family members before reaching this conclusion.

He next sent Margaret for an electro-encephalogram examination, the results of which showed no organic brain disease. He records that this test, whilst not confirming epilepsy, did not rule it out either. Margaret admitted to Cormack that she had suffered one of her dizzy bouts immediately prior to Nancy appearing at her door and she confirmed that, at the time she had killed Nancy, she had been going through a phase of irritability.

Cormack also observed Margaret's demeanour whilst in prison. He found she had *'behaved quite normally, slept soundly, taken her food, shown interest in her surroundings, associated with others and occupied herself in a satisfactory manner.'* He recorded that she had been clean and tidy in her habits, which we will see was a departure from her usual custom. Cormack did not know this, though, and cleanliness and orderly behaviour was something which was not just encouraged but was enforced in prison. Moreover, the prison facilities for personal ablution were undoubtedly better than those which Margaret had at home. Being served with regular meals was something she had not experienced since her mother had died. Little wonder, then, that she slept soundly and behaved normally.

Cormack commented that he found her conversation rational and he deduced she was *'of fair intelligence though not of high scholastic ability'*. He did, however, detect in her *'a degree of anxiety and emotional reaction',* though he qualified this by adding that it was *'quite in keeping with her present circumstances'*.

By *'present circumstances'*, presumably, he meant her imprisonment and the prospect of her imminent murder trial. Of course, he had not met her before her imprisonment, so he would have been unable to judge whether, and to what degree, she might have been suffering from anxiety and emotional reaction prior to the murder. He had not seen her at a time when her personal circumstances were desperate and deteriorating. Did he not realise that, in making this distinction so unscientifically, he was most likely condemning Margaret to death?

Margaret was able to give Cormack a good account of her past life and work record, and therefore he found *'her memory, reasoning and judgement unimpaired and she manifested no signs of mental illness, disorder or defect.'* He added that *'a physical examination failed to find any evidence of organic disease'*.

Cormack concluded that Margaret was simply passing through the menopause, and he opined that *'during this phase, women may be subject to many and varied symptoms, including vertigo, irritability and emotional disturbances.'*

That said, his overall diagnosis was: *'I am of the opinion that the accused, at the time of committing the act, was not suffering from such a defect of reasoning from disease of the mind as not to know the nature and quality of the act or that what she was doing was wrong. I consider she is fit to plead to the indictment and stand her trial.'*

Cormack had worked as a medic in the Prison System for around twenty years and so his medical opinion was respected, though he might have had some unorthodox ways of interpreting a prisoner's mental state and criminal inclinations.

Ten years earlier, for example, whilst serving as MO at London's Brixton Prison, he had co-authored a paper linking criminal behaviour with the surprisingly frequent incidence of criminals having eye pupils of different sizes. He records no such observation about Margaret's pupils.

The man of the house

As the police investigations revealed, Margaret's had been a difficult life thus far. From an unsettled and impoverished childhood, including a couple of years spent in a children's home, and witnessing her father's violent behaviour, as well as having to bear the twin stigmas of illegitimacy and gender 'dysphoria', Margaret had spent most of her adult life living with her mother.

Clearly, she had relied upon her mother to carry out all the necessary domestic tasks. Indeed, Margaret did not acquire any domestic skills herself and perhaps she thought it unmanly to do so. Margaret's only friend, Annie Cook [see Introduction and Chapter 6], would later explain that, following the death in 1943 of Margaret's dysfunctional but much-loved mother, Margaret had begun to neglect herself and her home.

Annie would tell Huggett and Berry that Margaret was incapable of cleaning or cooking for herself and that, from 1943, she had *'existed mainly on a diet of tea, beer and cigarettes'*. Also since 1943, her home circumstances had begun to fall into greater and greater decline.

In fact, Annie described Margaret's home as 'wick' – a Lancashire word meaning alive with lice or fleas. Annie added that, when the various investigating officers had left the house, they found that they, too, were 'wick'. This paints an even more vivid picture of Margaret's living conditions than does the police officer's description of 137 Bacup Road as *'absolutely filthy'*. It might also explain the reluctance of three police officers to spend much time in Margaret's house during their enquiries immediately following the murder.

Margaret's mother had not just provided her unmarried daughter with practical support, but with emotional support, too. In Huggett and Berry's words, Alice Dobson had known that, of all her many children, Margaret had been the *'odd man out'*, and yet, to the best of her limited abilities, Alice had loved Margaret as well, if not better than the rest of her exceptionally large brood.

It was Margaret who had stayed at home and lived with her mother until the age of thirty-seven. Margaret had been the breadwinner, in effect the man of the house, and Alice had been the housewife. In this respect, they had lived almost as a married couple. Alice's death, therefore, had left an enormous void in Margaret's life, both emotionally and practically.

In 1946, however, all that was to change. Indeed, Margaret's life would change irrevocably. According to Huggett and Berry, quite unexpectedly and against all the odds, this lonely and depressed middle-aged spinster would fall in love.

A portrait believed to be that of
the young Margaret Allen
(source unattributable)

Chapter 6 – The Lover?

'Vivacious, lively and essentially feminine – Huggett and Berry describing Annie Cook.

Sometime around 1946, Margaret Allen was to make the acquaintance of a young woman who would fill that void left by the death of her mother; a woman who would become her best friend – indeed her only friend – and would be the only person to support her following her arrest. Presumably because they were unfamiliar with the concept of transgenderism, Huggett and Berry had concluded that Margaret Allen was a lesbian. According to the two authors, for Margaret to have attracted such devoted friendship, she and Annie Cook must have become lovers.

Born Annie Tattersall on 16 January 1916, Annie was ten years younger than Margaret. The daughter of Harry Tattersall, a stoker at Rawtenstall's gas works, and his wife (also Annie, née Devonport), Annie was a cotton mill worker. Annie had only one sibling, a sister named Gladys, but both girls were remembered locally as being very good looking in their youth. They were slightly built and had lustrous brown hair, beautiful eyes and attractively sculpted cheekbones. Like Margaret, Annie did not have much education but had also started work at the age of twelve, as a half-timer in a mill.

In July 1939, 23-year-old Annie had married a local man, twenty-five-year old Willie Cook, a weaver's son and a coal bagger by occupation. Just weeks later, Willie had enlisted and gone off to war. On his return, however, irreconcilable differences between the couple had caused them to separate and Annie had decided to divorce him. Divorce was still an expensive process back then and was mainly the resort of the moneyed classes. Solicitors' fees were still beyond the reach of many ordinary people, so Annie had to save hard to secure her freedom from an unhappy and short-lived marriage.

Although the exact date and circumstances of Annie's and Margaret's first meeting are not recorded, Annie was living back at home with her parents at this time, at 15 Union Terrace, Rawtenstall, and was saving up to pay the solicitor's fees for her divorce petition. She had little choice but to live with her parents, since it is unlikely that, on a female textile worker's pay, she could have afforded to rent a place on her own. In those days, the practice of working folks house-sharing or taking in lodgers to help with the rent was common.

Huggett and Berry described the 39-year-old Annie, when they met her in 1955, as *'vivacious, lively and essentially feminine'*. She was *'slight and short, with attractive brown hair and a pleasantly soft speaking voice contrasting sharply with Bill Allen's deeper, masculine speech'*[24]. This would, of course, have been a speculative comparison, since Huggett and Berry never actually met Margaret Allen.

The two authors formed the impression that Annie was hard-working, practical and reliable, and also naturally kind and considerate. Given her disappointing experience of marriage, it is possible that Annie had been disinclined to rush into another heterosexual relationship when she met and befriended Margaret. Annie's demonstrably kind nature probably meant she was moved by Margaret's plight and had felt immediate sympathy for someone who was lonely and incapable of seeing to her own daily needs.

Annie was able to see beyond her new friend's off-putting outward appearance and was not embarrassed to be seen with her in public; nor was she fazed by the squalor of Margaret's home. Moreover, she was quite comfortable referring to her friend as 'Bill' instead of Margaret, and she did so throughout her 1955 interview with Huggett and Berry.

Once they had become acquainted, Margaret and Annie soon began seeing each other every evening after work. For more than two

---

[24] From 'Daughters of Cain' [by Huggett & Berry, Pan Books 1955].

years, they would meet at the same spot at the corner of Kay Street and Bacup Road and would go to a local pub. Sometimes their venue of choice would be the Ram's Head but most often it was the Ashworth Arms. This latter pub, named in honour of the aforesaid land- and mill-owning Ashworth family, was located on the Bacup Road, midway between their respective homes, and here they would while away evenings in each other's company, enjoying a leisurely glass of beer or two and a cigarette.

Annie often visited Margaret's house and she told Huggett and Berry: '*every Saturday morning for* [the past] *five months, I'd called for her, but I was in a hurry that morning* [the morning of the murder] *and arranged to meet her in the town.*' With the dubious benefit of hindsight, Annie felt that, had she called for Margaret that Saturday as she usually did, or had Margaret at least known that Annie's arrival at the house was imminent, the murder might never have happened. Annie's route into town would take her past Margaret's house anyway, so she must indeed have had some pressing business that morning, perhaps to do with finalising her divorce.

From time to time, Margaret would call on Annie at her parents' home on Union Terrace and, whenever she did, Annie's mother would welcome her in. *'Often, she arrived at our house just as we were going to sit down to dinner,'* Annie would later recall, *'and many's the time I've seen my mother put her own dinner in front of 'Bill' and make do with a sandwich herself.'*

Annie added that Mrs Tattersall would also slip her daughter's friend a few shillings whenever Margaret was on her uppers. Mrs Tattersall, too, must have found something very likeable in Margaret Allen.

The kindness shown to Margaret by Annie and her family is not just known by Annie's own account. The police interviewed Leonard Thomas, a clothing manufacturer's representative, who said that, in October 1947, Margaret had purchased from him, on credit, a raincoat, a pair of men's shoes and some men's trousers. The re-payments on the purchase amounted to four shillings a week and he collected these payments from a 'Mrs Tattersall' at 15 Union Terrace. He said the payments were up to date as at 21 August 1948, the week before Margaret's arrest.

This method of payment collection might have been a matter of mere convenience, had Margaret been working full time at this point.

However, this was not the case. Given that Margaret had been sitting at home, unemployed, for all of 1948 and had not herself paid any bill whatsoever since 1946, it seems more likely that Annie's mother was actually funding the re-payments on Margaret's clothing.

A friend in need

All in all, it seems Annie and her mother were regularly providing Margaret with food, clothing and occasionally cash too. Being Margaret Allen's friend cannot have been easy. Aside from the fact that their association would almost certainly have raised eyebrows and caused gossip, Annie told Huggett and Berry that Margaret was prone to periods of depression.

Annie recounted an incident which had occurred when she and Margaret had been having an argument. During this exchange, Annie had told Margaret she needed to pull herself together and find work. Fearing that Annie was trying to break up with her, alarmingly, Margaret had tried to gas herself. Annie had intervened and had wrested the gas pipe from Margaret's mouth to prevent her friend from committing suicide. Margaret's extreme reaction to the thought of losing Annie does suggest that her attachment to Annie went some way beyond friendship.

Annie would cook and clean for Margaret on occasions and had given her some curtains to make her drab and dirty home a little more cheerful. Annie also related that, when Margaret had fallen deeply into debt and had sold her gas cooker for £9, Annie had tried to persuade her to use that £9 to pay off her rent arrears. It seems, however, that Margaret did not share Annie's practical sense of priorities. Margaret would put that £9 towards a holiday trip for them both instead.

Escape from Rawtenstall

The Whitsun week of May 1948 was an especially glorious one. The weather was exceptionally hot and sunny, even in Lancashire, and the press were describing the phenomenon as 'a heat wave'. In fact, that week saw some of the best weather experienced in Lancashire since before the war, though it was to be followed by a wet and dismal summer.

Many of the factories and mills closed for Whitsun. Unsurprisingly, therefore, working-class folks headed en masse, by train or charabanc, for the seaside. Lancashire's Fylde coast had several excellent resorts, the most popular being Blackpool with its fine sands, Eiffel-inspired tower and the gaudy amusements of its 'Golden Mile'.

This was the heyday of the seaside boarding houses, with their strict rules administered by formidable landladies. Long the butt of northern comedians, these women were also the self-appointed guardians of public morals in the heady holiday atmosphere of the resort. Unmarried couples sharing rooms was frowned upon. Beds were solely for sleeping upon and guests were expected to remain out of doors all day, regardless of the weather, and were not permitted to return to their rooms until just before supper.

'Hanky Panky' (as Walter Greenwood, Lancashire-born author of 'Love on the Dole', would describe casual sexual liaison) was firmly discouraged. Nevertheless, in the hedonistic surroundings of Blackpool, stressed workers could unwind in the sea and on the sands. There was much fun to be had on the rides at the Pleasure Beach and romance could blossom on the dance floor of the Tower Ballroom.

Margaret and Annie took advantage of the unseasonably hot Whit week to join the crowds heading for Blackpool. When they checked into one of the boarding houses on Talbot Road[25], Margaret registered them as 'Mr and Mrs Allen'. It is unlikely that the landlady, Mrs Wheeler, would have mistaken them for a married heterosexual couple, especially since she would have seen Margaret's name on her ration book[26]. It is more likely that she thought they were just two women friends having a silly lark.

Whatever the case, they were accommodated seemingly without quibble. Their week in Blackpool may have been the first real holiday either of them had ever had, but it would certainly have represented a truly blissful escape for the two friends from dull working-class life in Rawtenstall.

Under police questioning, Annie confirmed that she and Margaret had shared a double-bedded room at the boarding house. Back in the 1940s, it was far from unusual for females, especially working-class women, to share a bed when on holiday or when staying over at a friend's house. Because of Margaret's insistence that she was a man, however, their sleeping arrangements in Blackpool would later be the subject of inordinate attention by the prosecution counsel.

The suggestion of a close physical relationship between the two women might have been a valid avenue of investigation, had it pointed

---

[25] This property is now a gay nightclub.
[26] Rationing was still in force, and ration books had to be surrendered to hotel or boarding house keepers to enable them to purchase food for guests' meals.

to a motive for the murder, or if it suggested Annie were either cognisant of or complicit in the crime, yet this was never alleged. One hopes it was more than just gratuitous sensationalism or an attempt at character blackening which led the prosecution counsel to go delving into this aspect of the women's friendship.

Friends or lovers?

So, was Annie and Margaret's relationship a physical one? When interviewed by police, Annie would claim Margaret had indeed requested sexual contact with her, but Annie insisted she had rebuffed Margaret's overtures. Given the prevailing attitudes back in 1948 to homosexual relationships, such a denial might perhaps be expected. However, the fact of their spending almost every evening together, which is perhaps more time than even the closest of platonic friends would spend in each other's company, suggests there was as much attachment on Annie's part as on Margaret's.

A letter Margaret later sent Annie from prison was signed 'with love', though of course this may not indicate anything beyond sisterly affection. Annie would never admit they were lovers, however, and nor was she known to be linked romantically with any other woman, either before or since. Like several other aspects of this case, this issue remains a matter for conjecture. Many local residents who were around at that time believe they were lovers, and, indeed, some of Annie's own family members have always assumed this was the case.

Huggett and Berry were certainly keen to present Margaret and Annie's association as being an intense lesbian love story. This helped the authors to make sense of subsequent events when Margaret's extreme passion would turn her hand to murder. If Annie and Margaret's relationship were not a romantic or sexual one, however, then Annie emerges from the story as an exceptionally kind and compassionate character, and a true friend indeed.

Margaret and Annie's favourite haunt, The Ashworth Arms on the
Bacup Road, is still in business today. (Author's photo).

15 Union Terrace, Rawtenstall, where Annie lived with her parents and where Margaret always found a warm welcome and a hot meal, is little changed today. (Author's photo).

Chapter 7 – The Means and the Motive

'The old bugger's crackers ... she nearly bit my damned head off!' –
Margaret Allen reportedly speaking of Nancy Chadwick.

Traditional and current investigation methods usually begin with detectives considering whether a suspect had the means, the motive and the opportunity of committing the crime. This, no doubt, would have been the approach adopted in the investigation into the murder of Nancy Chadwick.

The Means

Although at less than five feet in height, Margaret Allen was some four inches or so shorter than Nancy Chadwick, she was younger and probably stronger, having drilled with the Home Guard and worked as a labourer. Wielding a weapon, she would certainly have been physically capable of killing the 68-year-old.

Many households in the 1940s would have a coal hammer to hand for the purpose of breaking up the larger lumps of coal for the domestic grate. Coal hammer heads had one flat side and one pointed side, either of which could do serious damage. Margaret's coal store was situated just inside her front door, a couple of steps away from the scullery and off the tiny lobby. It was in this small, confined area that, according to her confession, an altercation had occurred, causing Margaret to beat Nancy to death using just such a coal hammer.

The physical evidence

The forensic evidence would support Margaret's admission to have attacked Nancy with a hammer, since it was found that Nancy had met her death from numerous blows to the head, such as might have been inflicted by a hammer. The forensics also found the deceased had been dragged some distance by the feet. Bloodied drag marks found on the pavement outside 137 Bacup Road, as well as the bloodstains found within the property, strongly suggested that this house was the scene of the crime.

Small blood spots were also found on some of Margaret's clothing and shoes. These, and samples of the bloodstains on the floor, were taken away for forensic testing. The blood group was identified as being of the most common British blood type: 'O-positive'. However, testing also revealed that *both* Nancy Chadwick and Margaret Allen were 'O-positive', so the blood could have come from either of them.

In 1948, before the development of DNA testing, blood type testing could eliminate suspects but it could not positively identify them. It is a matter of record that Margaret was experiencing erratic and unpredictable menstruation and was poor at both cleaning her home and maintaining personal hygiene. Her only place to wash was in her small kitchen, so the blood found on her clothing, shoes and on the wall might just have been her own.

Additionally, fibres were found upon a pair of Margaret's trousers and were found to be of the 'same type' as fibres from the deceased's coat. Disappointingly, however, no other clothing in Margaret's house seems to have been tested to see whether it, too, was of the 'same type' as these fibres. A single hair, said to be 'similar' to Nancy's, was also found on Margaret's trousers, but if any comparison was made with Margaret's own hair then this fact is not recorded.

A week after Margaret's arrest, a letter signed 'R. M. H.' was sent to the Chief Constable of Lancashire, Sir Archibald Hordern AFC, CBE, KPM. The letter reads: *'I am so glad this case is cleared up and only wish we could have the same luck in the case of the two boys[27].'* 'R.M.H.' was most probably R.M. Horne of the Metropolitan Police. He and Hordern had recently served together on a Home Office committee tasked with improving the effectiveness of detective work, especially in the use of forensic evidence. As a result, Horne, Hordern and other police

---

[27] Undoubtedly this referred to the case of the two Deanwater boys who had not been found at this time and never would be.

chiefs were placing increasing reliance on the physical forensic evidence in solving murders.

Forensic evidence would indeed play an increasingly important role in crime solving throughout the twentieth century, though, of course, the accurate and appropriate interpretation of such evidence is crucial. Forensics must always be considered together with other types of evidence, especially evidence relating to motive and opportunity. The most damning evidence against Margaret Allen, however, was not the forensics. It was her own admission of guilt.

No sooner had the police queried the presence of the stains, the blood-soaked ashes and the damp cleaning rag, than Margaret had confessed to the killing. She had earlier witnessed the police's lack of success in dredging the Irwell for any implement which might have been the murder weapon and so she knew no such weapon had been found. Yet, when challenged, she had immediately volunteered details of what she had used to kill Nancy and how she had disposed of it and concealed the body. It was as if she were bursting to unburden herself of her guilt.

That might be the case, or at least that is how the police's record of events suggests it happened. They record that she rolled over and confessed immediately when challenged. Perhaps, however, that is not how it happened. A rumour still persists in Rawtenstall that the police took Margaret to a nearby pub and got her drunk, to the point that she weakened and confessed, but this may not have been necessary.

An alternative possibility, though the scant notes on the police files do not reflect this, is that the admission actually emerged as a result of some fairly intense interrogation by detectives Woodmansey and Stevens. Police examination techniques during that era were certainly more heavy-handed than is permitted nowadays. It was not unknown for suspects to find themselves on the receiving end of intimidation, trickery and even the odd slap.

These were certainly the techniques for which Scotland Yard man DCI Capstick was known. Indeed, on the force, Capstick was known by the nickname 'Artful Charlie' because of his interviewing skills. John Woodmansey would have observed Capstick's infamous interrogation technique four months earlier whilst they worked together during the intense and pressurised, though ultimately unsuccessful investigation into the murder of young Jack Quentin Smith.

Would it even have taken very much pressure from two large police officers to get an ill-educated, vulnerable, depressed and fearful suspect like Margaret to confess?

The Motive?

Paying heed to local rumours that Nancy Chadwick had been in the habit of carrying large sums of money around with her, and in the absence of any readily discernible alternative, the detectives quickly concluded that robbery had been the most likely motive for the murder. Though Margaret denied this was so, she did admit to having checked Nancy's bag before disposing of it, too, in the river. She claimed she had found it contained very little money, though, of course, she would not have known this until after she had killed Nancy.

Huggett and Berry opined that, had Margaret been possessed of a feminine temperament, whatever disagreement she had with Nancy might have resulted in a slap being administered or crockery being thrown, but that it was Margaret's masculine nature which had caused her to reach for the hammer instead. Whether or not this is fair comment, the ferocity of the attack upon Nancy certainly suggests her killer must have been very, very angry. The damage done to Nancy went far beyond what was necessary to incapacitate her or even to kill her. So, was the motive likely to have been as straightforward as robbery?

Nancy's purse was never found. Some metal studs found in Margaret's downstairs grate, and suspected at first to be from a purse, were examined by the forensic expert who concluded that these were the fastenings from a shoe, not a purse. This is not as unlikely as it may seem, for it was a long-established working-class habit to burn worn-out leather shoes in domestic fires rather than throw them away. They burned slowly and gave out good heat. Some of the press reports, however, described those studs as being from a woman's purse, and that assertion was never corrected but has often been repeated.

No money was found stashed away at 137 Bacup Road and, apart from buying beers for herself and Annie on the day of the murder, Margaret was not seen to spend money on any big purchases between the time of the murder and her arrest. Nor is there any suggestion in the police files that she had made any deposits of cash in her bank account following the murder. One assumes the police would have checked this, albeit that it is not mentioned on file. When searched by Policewoman

Marjorie Dodds on 1st September, Margaret possessed only one pound, one shilling, one penny, two halfpennies and two farthings.

That Margaret was deeply in debt was not disputed. Her rent and utilities payments were greatly in arrears and she had several times been served with a notice to quit the house. She had ignored these notices and Greenbank Estates had taken no steps to evict her. Accommodation was very scarce immediately after the war, so either Greenbank were being kind to Margaret or perhaps people were not exactly queueing around the block for such woefully inadequate accommodation as 137 Bacup Road.

Margaret also owed money for groceries she had bought 'on tick',[28] and her insurance payments were overdue. She owed significant amounts to several local tradesmen, including a boot repairer. It seems odd that she should use a boot repairer, however, when one of her neighbours would later depose that, not only did Margaret repair her own boots, but her kindness extended to also repairing her neighbours' shoes, free of charge as a favour.

All in all, Margaret's debts at the time of her arrest amounted to £46. 0s. 11d,[29] and some of her debts and unpaid bills dated as far back as 1946. Surprisingly, however, the police discovered she had a savings account with a balance of £32.[30] It is odd that Margaret had been in possession of sufficient funds to pay off the bulk of her debts yet had failed to do so. It seems Margaret was as incompetent at managing her finances as she was at managing her domestic chores.

The rumours circulating about Nancy Chadwick's distrust of banks and having large sums of money about her person were repeated in the press. It was also reported that she was regularly to be seen sitting in public places such as parks counting out her money. One witness interviewed by police on this issue was Beatrice Haworth of 13a Longholme Road. This 59-year-old housewife, at whose home Margaret would claim she had once met Nancy, told police:

'I knew Mrs Chadwick. She was a miser. She would never open her purse. It was common knowledge she carried large sums of money in her bag. A few weeks ago, she told me she had put £40 in the bank.'

---

[28] Most small shopkeepers allowed regular customers to buy groceries on credit and settle up on pay day.
[29] Equivalent to £1,169 at today's values.
[30] Worth around £813 today.

This comment about the £40 does not seem to have been verified by the police, but it was established that Nancy was not always a truthful person. She had told some locals that her husband had died in World War One, which was certainly untrue. She also claimed to be able to predict the future using playing cards and tea leaves, but this was plainly a ruse enabling her to call on people to cadge cups of tea or meals. One of Nancy's tenants, Nellie Parry of 9 Mount Pleasant, also said of Nancy in her deposition:

'She was a very eccentric woman. Sometimes she had large amounts of money, sometimes just coppers. She last called for rent on 21 August at twelve noon. I gave her thirteen shillings, the fortnight's rent.'

Since Paddy Whittaker had said Nancy only collected her rents fortnightly, Nellie Parry's confirmation that Nancy had collected hers on 21 August suggests that, on the following Saturday – the day she was killed – Nancy would not have been collecting rent money. Therefore, she may not have had much money on her person, just as Margaret claimed.

A woman who would describe herself as Nancy's close friend, Mrs Mary Ellen Jordan, told police that Nancy was in fact more guarded about her wealth than the press reports suggested:

'It is not true what they said in the papers about Mrs Chadwick counting out her money in public places. She would never let people see what was in her purse out in the street and hardly ever in shops. She wanted people to think she had no money. She would wear old shoes even when she had new ones.'

Nancy's employer, Paddy Whittaker, was perhaps best placed to know the contents of Nancy's purse. He told police that, on 22 August, he had seen her transfer *'a pound or two'* from her old purse into the new purse her nephew had given her. He later said he had also seen her put *'two or three pounds'* in her purse on the day before her death.

Paddy also confirmed that, contrary to popular rumour, Nancy did trust banks and had regularly banked her money – and his – in an account in her name, which currently had a balance of £27. It was learned that she had recently spent £60 on house repairs, so the savings account was a little depleted at this time. Despite Beatrice Haworth's comments, there was no evidence to suggest Nancy had a large sum of money with her when she had left home on the morning of her death. That does not, of course, rule out the possibility that local people, including her killer, supposed that she had.

A more likely motive?

Despite the lack of any evidence that Margaret had relieved Nancy of more than a few coppers, the police seem to have stopped looking for any alternative reason for the murder or, indeed, for any alternative murderer. They had their suspect in custody and had a signed confession on the file, and that was enough to take the case to court. However, in the absence of any proof that Margaret had benefited financially from killing Nancy, the judge at her trial would later conclude that the killing of Nancy Chadwick had been a 'motiveless' crime.

There is a more obvious motive, however, and it is one which should have been apparent to the police from their witness statements, but it was either missed or, more likely, disregarded. It was Albert Einstein who famously said, that if the facts don't fit the theory, then one should change the facts. It seems that, in Margaret's case, the police actively concealed facts which did not fit their theory.

The police reports describe Margaret's home circumstances as 'very poor' and her rented house as being 'absolutely filthy'. This was partly due to her lethargy and lack of domestic skills, but was probably also due to the fact that 137 Bacup Road had never been intended to be a residential property and had not been well maintained. As a former toll booth and later a lock-up for criminals, it lacked even the most basic facilities. During Margaret's occupation, it also seems to have suffered from landlord neglect.

Once her new, hard-working and practical friend Annie began to call upon her, it may be that Margaret had begun to feel ashamed of the place. By her own account, Annie had found the house dirty and infested with lice, so much so, that the police officers had inadvertently taken lice with them on leaving the premises. Presumably, Margaret, too, was infested with lice.

There is, however, reliable evidence to suggest that, after five years of living in some squalor, something had happened in Margaret's life to make her consider moving out of this semi-derelict and unsuitable property and seek somewhere better to live. That something may have been her relationship with Annie.

Whilst it might be supposed that Margaret's straightened financial circumstances would make it difficult for her to afford better accommodation, this is actually not the case. Indeed, there is evidence that, on the very day of the murder, she was actively seeking to rent a better quality of house – one of the two-bedroom Mount Pleasant cottages owned by none other than Nancy Chadwick.

A dream of a better life?

54-year-old Fred Taylor of 65 Hardman Avenue, told police:

'I know the accused who worked on the buses with my daughter [Nellie Parry] and has visited my house. At 0925 on Saturday 28 August, I met her coming up Hardman Avenue. She said 'I've been to Mrs Chadwick's to see about an exchange of a house, but I've made an appointment to see her on Monday after she's seen her own tenant.' We walked along together and chatted. She said 'the old bugger's crackers'.'

Fred's daughter, Nellie Parry, one of Nancy's tenants up at Mount Pleasant, confirmed this. She told police:

'I am the daughter of Fred Taylor of 65 Hardman Avenue. On Saturday 28 August, I was talking to my father who said he had been chatting to Maggie Allen and she said she had been up to see 'Pushem'[31] about changing houses, but said 'Pushem' had nearly bit her damned head off.'

Was it possible that unemployed Margaret could even have afforded a better house? Yes, it was. Margaret's rent on the old and decayed former police lock-up down on the busy Bacup Road was six shillings and four pence a week. Nancy was charging seven shillings and ten pence a week for each of her two-bedroom terraced cottages, which were situated in an elevated location in a quieter and more desirable residential street with lovely views.

At the time of the murder, although unemployed, Margaret was in receipt of eleven shillings a week in public assistance payment and twenty-six shillings a week national health assistance. With an income

---

[31] The police file is annotated to the effect that 'Pushem' was a nickname the bus conductresses had for Nancy Chadwick, perhaps due to her impatient pushing of slow passengers queuing ahead of her to board the bus.

of thirty-seven shillings a week, she could indeed have afforded the seven shillings and ten pence weekly rent on one of Nancy's properties, and, moreover, Fred Taylor had confirmed this was her stated purpose in making contact with Nancy on the day Nancy was killed.

Furthermore, the witness Beatrice Haworth told police that Margaret had been looking for Nancy one week before the murder, albeit that Margaret appeared not to know Nancy's name. Like the other bus conductors, Margaret probably only knew Nancy as *'Pushem'*, and she probably knew only vaguely where Nancy lived, having seen where she boarded and left the bus. Beatrice described how Margaret had called at her (Beatrice's) home on Saturday 21 August – wet through, since it was raining heavily – to ask if Beatrice knew where to find *'the woman who kept house for the old man on Hall Carr'*.

Allegedly, Margaret told Beatrice she held a parcel for him, given to her by the old man's son when she was visiting Haslingden. Beatrice further stated that, the following week, she had asked Nancy whether Paddy had received his parcel, but Nancy had known nothing about any parcel. Clearly, the story about the parcel was simply a ruse on Margaret's part to find out where Nancy lived, but why was Margaret seeking out Nancy?

Another witness, Phoebe Evelyn Payne, who lived next door to Nancy and Paddy, stated she had seen Margaret visit the Whittaker house on Sunday 22 August, and said it was the only time she had ever seen Margaret there. This would suggest, therefore, that Margaret did not really know Nancy but nevertheless had an urgent reason for wanting to track her down, even to the extent of going out in heavy rain to look for her.

These statements by witnesses Haworth and Payne, however, contradict that made by Paddy Whittaker, who had told police Margaret had visited Nancy twice some two to three weeks prior to the murder. This suggests Margaret *had* been aware of Nancy's address before she had visited Beatrice to ask for it. Could both women have been mistaken about the dates on which they had seen Margaret visit Nancy? It seems unlikely that, if mistaken, both women would have come up with the same weekend.

Moreover, it would make no sense for Margaret to be enquiring about Nancy's address if, as Paddy alleged, she had already been there. Also, if Margaret had evil intent towards Nancy, then asking for her address would have drawn attention to her unnecessarily. Was it Paddy,

71

described by police as an *'aged witness'*, who was mistaken? Alternatively, might the police have put words into Paddy Whittaker's mouth in a bid to establish a stronger acquaintance between the victim and her killer?

If Beatrice Haworth is to be believed, Margaret was almost certainly lying about her reasons for wanting to find Nancy. If she had really been given a parcel for *'the old man'*, surely the parcel would have had the man's name upon it, or his son would at least have told her the recipient's name? Perhaps Margaret simply did not want Beatrice to know her business and so she concocted the story about the parcel. She knew Fred Taylor fairly well, though, and so may have felt more comfortable telling him of her plan to speak to Nancy about renting one of her houses.

Though Nancy was the one with the reputation as a scrounger, it seems it was also Margaret's habit from time to time to try and obtain money from people she knew only slightly. Beatrice Haworth also said that Margaret had called on her again on Friday 27 August, the day before Nancy's murder. This time, Margaret had claimed she had been contacted by the police, informing her that her sister was ill in Manchester Royal Hospital and so, naturally, Margaret wanted to visit her. Margaret told Beatrice she had a postal order but could not change it, so, allegedly, Beatrice's daughter had given Margaret two shillings, but these ladies would see neither Margaret nor the two shillings again. Beatrice's daughter was not asked by police to corroborate this statement.

Was Margaret really seeking new accommodation? If not, why else would she be seeking out a woman who was known to be a miser? Apparently, she had found a soft touch in Beatrice's daughter, but it is unlikely she would have expected to borrow money from Nancy who had an established reputation for meanness. Fred Taylor's statement that Margaret was looking to rent one of Nancy's cottages makes perfect sense. Margaret was greatly in arrears with the rent on her current home. Exchanging houses and landlords might have offered her an escape from this situation. Would Margaret need a two-bedroom dwelling, though? Well, yes, she would if it had been her intention to share the cottage with best friend Annie.

Having been married and been used to running her own household, Annie was back living at her parents' home again following her separation. She had been in continuous and full-time employment for the previous ten years at least and currently worked at a local mill, so she sounds like a fairly independent young woman to be back home living with Mum and Dad. Living at home thus far, though, had enabled her to save up for a divorce and had perhaps given her sufficient savings with which she might set herself up a little more independently.

If, as Annie claimed, she was spending every evening in Margaret's company anyway, and was regularly cleaning and cooking for Margaret, perhaps the idea of their moving in together had occurred and appealed to the friends. It certainly made good economic sense. Were Annie to have contributed towards Margaret's rent and utilities, the couple could have lived together quite comfortably. It seems a strong possibility, therefore, that, with Annie's practical influence, Margaret was seeking to make some long overdue changes and improvements in her home life.

A dream that slipped away?

Nancy Chadwick, however, had a reputation as an impatient, frugal and eccentric sponger. It seems that she also had no compunction about taking financial advantage of her vulnerable and dependent employer. Her own nephew described how his 'abnormal' aunt would frequent jumble sales where she bought second hand clothes – the typically old-fashioned clothes of the Victorian age into which she had been born. She may have held typically Victorian opinions and attitudes, too.

Nancy was a member of the congregation of St Mary's, Rawtenstall – an evangelical Christian church, the doctrine of which was opposed to homosexuality. It seems unlikely, therefore, that Nancy would have approved of Margaret's appearance and lifestyle. She might well have been affronted at the idea of taking on someone like Margaret as a tenant. Nancy may not have held back when expressing her revulsion at Margaret's suggestion that she and Annie should occupy one of her houses, if that was indeed what Margaret had discussed with her.

It is wholly plausible that the reason for Margaret's comment *'the old bugger's crackers'*, and the reason why *'Pushem'* had *'nearly bit her damned head off'*, was that Nancy had volubly expressed her aversion to the prospect of someone she perceived to be a cross-dressing lesbian living together with a divorcee in one of *her* properties. Such a thing may well have offended her evangelical principles. Margaret's comment to Fred Taylor suggests Nancy had, indeed, sent her away with a flea in her ear over something and, in the light of Fred's statement regarding

Margaret's stated purpose in visiting Nancy, a refusal to rent her a house would seem to be a more reasonable explanation for their falling out.

Did Margaret dream of a new life with the lovely Annie in a nice, clean cottage in a quiet, respectable street, and did Nancy stand in the way of that dream? Could it be that Margaret had come away from Nancy's house bitterly disappointed at being rejected and having had her head bitten off? Might cantankerous Nancy have followed her home in order to bring her taunts and insults to Margaret's own front door?

Is it feasible that, when Nancy had paid Margaret a return visit that fateful morning, she had stood just inside Margaret's door and told her exactly what she thought of her and her association with Annie? If this were the case, would this have been sufficient to push over the edge an already irritable, depressed and moody menopausal woman; sufficient to induce her to yield to impulse and strike Nancy ten times with the coal hammer which she found immediately to hand?

Well, clearly, this was an unplanned murder and, unarguably, the savage nature of the injuries inflicted upon Nancy was indicative of rage rather than pre-meditated robbery with violence. If, on the other hand, the police's theory was true – that Margaret had heard rumours of Nancy's supposed stash of cash and had actually planned to kill and rob her – then going around beforehand telling neighbours she was looking for Nancy seems a pretty stupid thing to do.

In her statements to police, Margaret herself did not mention the business of the proposed house exchange and, though Fred Taylor revealed this in his statement, Margaret was not questioned about it. For the police to have ignored this important evidence of a disagreement between killer and victim on the very day of the murder – evidence which was so relevant to a possible motive – is both surprising and disappointing. Moreover, the police decided to completely disregard Fred's and Nellie's statements and, more inexcusably, to withhold them from the defence. But why *did* Nancy pay Margaret a return visit so soon after their meeting and possible altercation in Hardman Avenue?

A sweetener?

In her own statement, Margaret told the police that the reason Nancy had come to her house on the day she died was because she had promised to get Nancy some extra sugar. Margaret would have had to obtain this via the black market, since it was still severely rationed at the time. It is this story about the sugar, however, which the police ran with as being the reason for Nancy's visit to Margaret's house on the morning she was killed. They never questioned Margaret's ability to obtain extra sugar rations, nor asked why she should even contemplate providing sugar to an *'old bugger'* whom she considered to be *'crackers'*. They concluded the sugar was a lure to bring Nancy and her cash to Margaret's lair.

Though another neighbour would mention Margaret having repaired her and other neighbours' shoes free of charge as a favour, neither she nor anyone else suggested Margaret had ever offered to obtain black market produce for them, or that she might even have had the contacts to enable her to do so. If, however, Margaret really had invited Nancy to her home on a false promise of giving her sugar, this might have been a deliberate ruse with a purpose other than robbery.

The promise of sugar may have been a hastily concocted and ill thought out idea; an inducement to persuade Nancy to change her mind about renting her the cottage. Margaret had not expected to see Nancy again until their pre-arranged meeting on the Monday, so she may have thought she could obtain some sugar before then, from the Tattersalls, perhaps. The promise of 'a sweetener' might, however, have tempted Nancy, even after their alleged falling out, to pay her an immediate return visit. The promise of such a scarce comestible would indeed have been a strong incentive for her to walk the half mile to 137 Bacup Road so soon after Margaret had visited her.

If this were the case, perhaps, when unexpectedly confronted by Nancy in the lobby of her own home, Margaret had no option but to confess that she did not actually have any sugar to give her. It might have been the natural reaction of a reputedly cantankerous old woman to react by spelling out, in no uncertain terms, what 'an abomination' she considered Margaret to be and why, sugar or no sugar, she would not entertain the idea of taking her on as a tenant.

It was unfortunate that Nancy was standing in that tiny, confined space just inside Margaret's front door as, towering four inches or so above Margaret, she probably spoke her mind bluntly. It was equally unfortunate that, despite it being August and unlikely that a coal fire would have been needed, nevertheless there was a coal hammer so close to hand. This was probably because, as we shall see, Margaret had just been using it to mend a pair of shoes for a neighbour.

So why on earth did Margaret not mention to the police the proposed house exchange as being the reason she had sought out Nancy?

If this were indeed the case, why did she not say she had been sorely provoked and offended by Nancy? Surely, this might have gone some way towards mitigating her violent attack on Nancy? It might have made Margaret seem less of a monster. Why did she mention only the promised sugar as the reason for their meeting? Could this have been because she did not want to disclose her reasons for seeking a bigger home? Might she have wished to keep Annie's name out of the affair, to prevent closer inspection of their relationship, and thereby preserve her friend's reputation? It might explain why Margaret said, and would continue to say nothing in her own defence.

There is, of course, no firm evidence that this was Margaret's motivation, but it makes much more sense than Margaret's explanation of her murderous rage having arisen simply out of *'one of my funny moods'*. Margaret's irritable menopausal mood may have been what led to her losing control once she began wielding the hammer, but something must have been said or done to have sparked off the assault in the first place. Did *'Pushem'* start pushing and prodding Margaret in the constricted and claustrophobic lobby of her own home? Did she continue the argument that had started up on Hardman Avenue? As Margaret told police, *'she seemed to insist on coming in'*. This seems a feeble explanation for what triggered a brutal murder.

If their argument had really come about because Nancy had refused to rent one of her houses to Margaret, would that be sufficient cause to enrage Margaret? Surely, she could have simply found another house to rent, couldn't she? Well, no, she couldn't have. Housing was extremely scarce in the immediate post-war period. There had been no house building since before the war and very little before that during the economically depressed 1930s.

There was very limited council accommodation available in the 1940s, and much of this was being allocated to returning servicemen who were now ready to settle down and start families, with the encouragement of the post-war government. As a single woman who had only lived in the town since 1943, Margaret would not have been placed high on the council house waiting list if, indeed, she even qualified. If word had got out about a privately rented property about to become available, Margaret would have had to move fast. This would be a feasible explanation for why she was out, in pouring rain, trying to find someone she scarcely knew – property owner Nancy Chadwick.

Then there is the seemingly insignificant statement by Nancy's nephew, William Barnes, that Nancy had called at his house three times during the week before her death but had not managed to catch him at home. Barnes had told the inquest into her death that she had wished to see him about something in particular, yet it seems he was not asked what that was.

At that time, Barnes was living in Ashworth Buildings at Higher Cloughfold. These were small and rundown back-to-backs built in the 1840s. However, Barnes was planning to marry the following summer. Indeed, his marriage would be brought forward for the usual reason of the bride's pregnancy. It is possible that, if one of Nancy's tenants was planning to vacate one of her houses, Nancy might have intended to offer the Mount Pleasant property to William and his bride to rent. Or, instead of leaving him *a little money* as he was expecting, she may even have intended to gift the house to the couple.

This, too, is wild speculation, of course, but if it were her intention, it might explain why she had been calling repeatedly on William. If the police ever asked William Barnes why his aunt had been so eager to see him prior to her death, they did not record his answers on file. Whatever the case, given the chronic housing situation of the day, there would have been no shortage of takers for Nancy's houses, especially since they were good houses and well located. Nancy could certainly have been choosy when selecting tenants. She did not need to take on as a tenant someone she did not know or did not like.

As the case files show, though, the police not only discounted, but actually withheld Fred's and Nellie's evidence. However, this was not just because it went against what they had decided was a convenient motive for the murder. In fact, it was because Fred's and Nellie's evidence, along with that of numerous other witnesses, suggests Margaret did not even have the *opportunity* of committing the murder.

Nancy's inheritance. The houses on Mount Pleasant today. (Author's photo).

Chapter 8 – The Opportunity

'I saw a man and a woman come out of the entry at the end of the cottages. I recognised her as Mrs Chadwick.' – Statement of Emily Whittaker of Fall Barn Crescent.

As well as means and motive, another critical factor to be determined in a murder case is whether the suspect actually had the opportunity of committing the crime. Investigators have to determine whether the suspect could, or could not have been present at the crime scene at the time the murder took place. Establishing this, of course, relies on knowing the precise time of death.

Several indicators are normally taken into account when determining the time of death of a murder victim. Dr Kay, the local physician who attended the scene very shortly after discovery of the corpse, had checked the body's temperature and felt for the presence of rigor mortis. He reported that the body was cold and that there was *'some stiffening of the limbs'*. He would then have noted those injuries which were obvious to him without his having to remove any of the victim's clothing. Accordingly, he recorded one deep laceration visible upon the scalp, the hair being matted with blood, and also bloodstains on the hands and forearms, as well as the presence of some ashes on the clothing.

Another way in which time of death *could* have been assessed, would have been by checking the stomach contents, to see when the digestion process and other bodily functions might have ceased. This would not normally be done at the roadside, but at a full post-mortem, conducted in more clinical surroundings. However, the state of digestion would only have been significant if the time the victim had consumed her last meal were known, and in Nancy's case this was never established.

It was pathologist Dr Gilbert Bailey who later conducted the post mortem on Nancy. He examined the body for further signs of injury. He found seven incised lacerations of the scalp in total, each extending to around one-inch long. There were a number of fractures all over the skull, all coming from different angles, suggesting a frenzied attack which continued as Nancy either dodged the blows or fell down. Dr Bailey declared that the cause of death was shock brought about by haemorrhaging from the scalp wounds.

Writing in Law and Order Magazine in 2007, Vernon J. Geberth, an experienced homicide and forensic consultant for the Police Department of New York, where violent murder is a far more common occurrence, said:

'Time is one of the most important factors of consideration in a murder case. It may very well convict a murderer, break an alibi or eliminate a suspect.'

Geberth, an acknowledged expert in his field, explains that rigor mortis – the post mortem stiffening of a corpse – begins three to four hours after death and is complete in eight to twelve hours. Police files record that, when Dr Kay examined the body of Nancy Chadwick at four fifteen that morning, some twenty minutes after its discovery, he determined that the victim had been dead about eight to ten hours, yet he reported only *'some stiffening of the limbs'*, not complete rigor mortis.

Perhaps Dr Kay was influenced in his assessment of time of death by the presence of post-mortem lividity, the purplish coloration of the skin caused by pooling of blood in that part of the body which has lain lowermost. Geberth holds that lividity becomes 'fixed' eight to ten hours after death. The deceased was found lying face-down in the roadway, and the police photographs taken at the scene, although black and white and too disturbing to be reproduced here, show her face to be darkly discoloured.

Geberth advises, however, that lividity may be affected by the body being moved *within* eight hours of death, but, if the body should be moved *more* than eight hours after the death it will have no effect on the appearance of lividity. The degree of lividity Dr Kay observed may have led him to assume either that Nancy had died at that spot – though the walking bus drivers' statements would rule this out, and it ought to have occurred to him that it was unlikely she could have lain in that major thoroughfare, unnoticed, for as long as eight or ten hours, – or that Nancy had died elsewhere whilst lying in the same position (ie face-down) as she was when found.

Detectives look for forensic clues at the spot where Nancy was found
(image courtesy of Peter Fisher)

Perhaps, in declaring with certainty the time of death to be eight to ten hours before the discovery, he failed to consider the possibility that her body had been moved to that spot, not immediately after death, but quite a long time afterwards? Perhaps, as a family GP, Dr Kay was not used to examining persons who had died by other than natural causes?

Forensic expert Dr Geberth's findings on post-mortem lividity warn that this may also be affected by other factors, such as the victim having lost a lot of blood, in which case there would be little or no coloration of the skin, or if the actual cause of death were heart failure or asphyxia, in which case there would be deep purple coloration. Either of these factors would be critical in assessing time of death. Unfortunately, the post mortem report on Nancy Chadwick does not go into such detail.

Whilst the massive injuries to Nancy's head were obvious to all, we do not know whether Dr Bailey considered the possibility of Nancy having suffered heart failure or asphyxiation during the assault. If she had done so, this might account for the combination of deep purple coloration with only partial stiffening of the limbs, and might suggest she had not been dead as long as Dr Kay estimated.

There was little blood at the place where the body was found – another factor which ought to have suggested to Dr Kay (as it did to driver Joe Unsworth) that Nancy had died elsewhere. Whether or not it did occur to Dr Kay, it did not cause him to reconsider his estimate of time of death. It was not until three days later that bloodstains would be found at Margaret's house, but by then Margaret had made at least some attempt to clear them up, and so the degree of blood loss could not be estimated or taken into account in establishing time of death.

Rawtenstall-based Police officer Stanley Marsden, who was on the scene fairly soon after the body's discovery, is on record as saying that, after examining the cadaver, Dr Kay told him the victim had been dead for ten hours, rather than eight to ten hours. It is not clear why Dr Kay amended his assessment slightly, but, within these estimates, Dr Kay's opinion was that death would have occurred sometime between six o'clock and eight o'clock on the Saturday *evening*. Strangely, this estimate of time of death is some ten to thirteen hours later than that suggested by Margaret Allen, who claimed Nancy had arrived at her house at around 9.20 on the Saturday *morning* and had been killed very soon after.

Margaret would tell police that all the clocks in her house were broken. The list of her possessions does not include a wristwatch, so her main means of knowing the time would have been by tuning in to her wireless or listening out for the chiming of the clock at St Mary's church. Whilst one might, therefore, expect her estimate of the time to be only approximate, she ought surely to have known whether she killed Nancy in the morning or in the evening. Is it possible that Nancy, having suffered such severe head injuries, and having been left lying in Margaret's coal cellar, could have remained alive for twelve hours or more before finally expiring? That, too, seems most unlikely, given her age and the seriousness of her wounds.

The time of death would have been a crucial factor in identifying Nancy's killer, as it is in any case of murder, so the significant and unresolved discrepancy between Dr Kay's estimate and Margaret's statement ought to have been very carefully investigated. However, this was just one of many serious inconsistencies which would emerge but which would never be resolved.

Nancy's movements

Nancy's employer, Paddy Whittaker, said Nancy had left his house at around 10.30 am that Saturday 28 August – a good hour after Margaret alleged she had killed her. It should be borne in mind, though, that one of the detectives who interviewed him had added to his interview notes: *'aged witness, recollection not good'*. However, a string of other witnesses would come forward to tell police they had seen Nancy at various places around the town all through that day and into late evening. Here is a list of those sightings in time order:

1. Catherine Walsh's house was at the corner of Yarraville street and Fall Barn Crescent and from there, she said in her statement, it was possible to see anyone passing to get to Fall Barn railway crossing and the Bacup road, since this was the only route down to those points [from the Hall Carr Estate]. At about **10 am**, she had seen Nancy Chadwick coming down Fall Barn Crescent from the direction of her home and heading towards Fall Barn river crossing. Catherine confirmed she knew Nancy Chadwick well and also knew Margaret Allen and was aware where each of them lived, though she had not seen Margaret at all that Saturday.

2. Witness Herbert Smith, who knew Nancy because she would call at his house to cadge a cup of tea, said he had seen her at **11am** crossing the footbridge which led from Cloughfold to the Bacup Road. This was one hour later than Catherine Walsh had seen Nancy travelling in the same direction along the same route.

3. James Wogden, of 18 Peter Street, said he had seen Nancy at **1.10 pm** crossing the brook at Longholme level crossing [further down the Bacup Road towards the town] at which time she was alone.

4. Local woman Bertha McGarrigan had seen Nancy in Woolworths store in the town at **2pm**.

5. Robert Murphy, a railway signalman, had seen Nancy at Fall Barn railway crossing at **5.30 pm.**

6. Nellie Parry, the aforementioned tenant of Nancy, lived at 9 Mount Pleasant, and her father lived near Nancy at 65 Hardman Avenue, so she knew Nancy very well. Nellie said she had seen Nancy at **6pm** walking away from her [Nancy's] house down Hardman Avenue, carrying some ration books.

7. Arthur Wogden, of 1 Union Terrace, had also seen Nancy at around **8.20pm**, walking alone up Bury Road towards Newhallhey Bridge.

8. Emily Whittaker (no relation to Paddy Whittaker) of 39 Fall Barn Crescent said she was walking back from a bus stop on the Bacup Road and turned into Fall Barn Close at around **10.25 pm** at which time she had seen Nancy Chadwick, whom she knew well, emerge from an entry. She said Nancy was accompanied by a man whom Mrs Whittaker did not know. Mrs Whittaker had bid Nancy 'Good night' and, though Nancy did not return her greeting, the man did.

This was the last reported sighting of Nancy on the day of her death and it suggests she was alive and well more than twelve hours after Margaret Allen claimed she had killed her, and between two and a half and four and a half hours after the time of death estimated by Dr Kay. Mrs Whittaker said the man she had seen with Nancy had been linking arms with her, was muttering to her and, judging by his speech, appeared to have been drinking.

She described him as 'elderly', which she then qualified as being aged around forty to fifty (!), and 'tallish' – compared to Nancy, whom she guessed to be around five feet four inches tall – thick set, with broad shoulders and wearing a dark suit and cap. From this description, clearly this 'man' was not the barely five-feet-tall Margaret Allen, whom witnesses would say was out and about that day, hatless and wearing an overcoat.

Emily Whittaker's statements may be given some credence, as she also said Nancy had on a grey coat and a dark hat and carried a shopping bag in front of her. This description of the deceased's clothing also corresponded more or less with 'Paddy' Whittaker's account of what he last saw Nancy wearing, except that the dark hat was in fact a black antimacassar worn as a headscarf. Emily's description of the clothing also tallied with the clothing later found on the body, albeit that, by then, the scarf was missing.

84

There were, therefore, eight witnesses besides Paddy Whittaker who claimed to have seen Nancy Chadwick out and about on the Saturday *after* the time Margaret Allen alleged she had killed her. However, the police apparently decided to ignore these witnesses. Moreover, an unsigned note on the police file boldly states:

'Mr Taylor's* evidence does not tally with the statement of the accused, so he is wrong. Fred Wilcock** is also wrong'.

Messrs Taylor and Wilcock had given statements (see the following) regarding Margaret's movements on that day. This shows that the police arbitrarily dismissed their statements out of hand because they did not accord either with Margaret's confession or with Dr Kay's estimate of time of death.

Margaret's movements

Even more confusion arose with regard to Margaret Allen's movements on Saturday 28 August.

1. Fred Taylor* claimed to have met Margaret coming down Hardman Avenue away from Nancy's house at precisely **09.25** that morning, which is around the time Margaret claimed Nancy was lying dead back at her (Margaret's) house. 137 Bacup Road was about half a mile from 81 Hardman Avenue and it would take an average walker around five to ten minutes to cover that downhill walk.

Taylor said that, when he had seen Margaret on Hardman Avenue, she was wearing a navy-blue overcoat with two side pockets and navy-blue trousers but no hat. Other witnesses would confirm this was what they had seen Margaret wearing that day, except that all the other witnesses described her coat as a fawn mackintosh. Taylor had not seen her up that way in some time, so he had jokingly enquired if she was lost.

Taylor said he had read in the press Margaret's claim that Nancy Chadwick had been at her (Margaret's) house at nine thirty that morning, but he insisted that could not be true. He knew Margaret and he was adamant he had been walking and talking with her up at Hardman Avenue. He was also adamant about the time.

2. Paddy Whittaker claimed to have risen at 0830 and said Nancy went out at about **1030**. He specifically said no-one had called at his house that

morning. Was Margaret lying to Fred Taylor about having called on Nancy? If not to see Nancy, why else would Margaret be in Hardman Avenue that morning? The police found Paddy's recollection was *'not good'*. Was he perhaps mistaken or might he have forgotten that Margaret had called? Perhaps it was only on the morning of the murder that Margaret had called, and not *'two or three weeks earlier'*, as this *'aged witness'* had told police? These discrepancies were never resolved.

3. Margaret Ann Evans, who lived just around the corner from Margaret Allen, at 7 Fall Barn Fold, told police:

*'At **lunchtime** on Saturday 28 August, I went to Margaret Allen's house and asked her if she'd heel a pair of my shoes. 'All right, cock, will do' she said. At **2.30**, she came to my door and brought the re-heeled shoes. She wouldn't take any money from me for it.'*

Although Evans did not give the precise time at which she had left her shoes with Margaret, her evidence suggests Margaret had spent that lunchtime up until 2.30 repairing the shoes. It is possible that Margaret was using the coal hammer to re-heel the shoes, and this may be why it was close at hand when Nancy called.

4. Bus conductor Fred Wilcock** also made a deposition regarding Margaret Allen's whereabouts on Saturday 28 August. He claimed he knew Margaret well, presumably from their time working on the buses together, and said he had seen her walking into town along the Bacup Road that evening at **7.55 pm** as he was on his way to the town's cinema. He described her as wearing dark trousers and a fawn-coloured, belted mackintosh. She was hatless and was distinctive because of her short haircut. He said they had greeted each other with a cheery 'hello', so he was in no doubt that it was Margaret. The main reason the police decided to discount Wilcock's account was because Margaret's sister would say [below] that Margaret was at her house from **4.30** until **9 pm** that evening, which, if true, entirely contradicts Wilcock's statement.

5. Mrs Lily Pickup of Ash Street, Cloughfold, gave an account of having spent time with her husband George and Margaret Allen at the Ashworth Arms on the evening of Saturday 28 August. She had seen Margaret arrive at the pub at around **9 or 9.15 pm.** Margaret had joined the couple

at their table and had engaged in conversation with them about the dubious quality of the beer lately. Lily said Margaret was still there chatting to George at **9.55** when she (Lily) had popped out to buy some chips at the local fish and chip shop. On her return to the pub, sometime later, Lily had seen Margaret leaving and walking towards the centre of Rawtenstall. At that time, she noted, Margaret was wearing dark slacks and a fawn coloured, belted raincoat but no hat.

6. 24-year-old Bridget Peel (née Melvin), was the wife of Harry Peel, son of Margaret's elder sister, Mary Alice Peel. Bridget told police that Margaret Allen had called on her at her home, 111 Plantation Street, Bacup, at about **1.30** on the afternoon Nancy was murdered. At a time when another witness had said Margaret was at home repairing shoes, Margaret was now alleged to have been over three miles away in a different town.

7. Bridget's mother-in-law, Margaret's sister Mary Alice Peel, was interviewed next and confirmed she lived next door to her son Harry and daughter-in-law Bridget, at 113 Plantation Street, Bacup. Mary Alice told police that Margaret and their mother used to live near each other in Bacup but that, following their mother's death, Margaret had gone to live at 137 Bacup Road, Rawtenstall. Since moving there, Mary Alice said, Margaret only came back to visit Mary Alice every two or three months.

Mary Alice went on to say that, at **4.30 pm** on 28 August, she had returned from a shopping trip to Rochdale with her daughter Mrs Annie Melvin[32]. As they reached the house, Margaret had appeared, emerging from Bridget's house, and had followed them next door into number 113, where Mary Alice made her a cup of tea. Mary Alice said Margaret, who kept her coat on, sat there talking, smoking and playing with Annie Melvin's baby, until about **9pm**. Mary Alice confirmed Margaret had been wearing her navy slacks, a blue striped shirt and collar with a tie, a navy blazer and a dirty, fawn-coloured, belted mackintosh.

Mary Alice also said that, during their conversation that evening, Margaret had asked to borrow thirty-five shillings for train fare to

---

[32] Mary Alice's son Harry and daughter Annie had married two siblings surnamed Melvin.

London. Margaret had told Mary Alice that a little boy[33] who had stayed with her as an evacuee during the war, had been hurt in an accident and was in a London hospital, so she wished to visit him. Mary Alice did not have that much money on her but had given Margaret half a crown, in return for which Margaret had given her a haircut. This would suggest Margaret had gained little if any money from killing Nancy.

8. 38-year-old gas works employee William George Warwick said he had set off walking from Bacup to Rawtenstall at around **1am** on Sunday 29 August and, almost an hour later, as he was passing Fall Barn, he had heard footsteps coming along Fall Barn towards the Bacup road. As he turned into the Bacup road, he heard the footsteps also turning into the Bacup road, and then heard the door of Margaret Allen's house, which was just six yards away from him, open and close again.

He said he did not notice any light on in that house and, shortly after this, he heard the clock at St Mary's church strike **2 am**, so by this he was able to pinpoint the time. He had come forward to tell the police this, he said, because he had read in the press a statement by Margaret Allen that she had been asleep all that night and had not been disturbed when Nancy's body had been dumped outside her door, but he knew this to be untrue. He was certain that it had been Margaret Allen's door which had opened and that this was where the footsteps had entered.

It seems more likely that in saying 'as I turned into the Bacup Road', Warwick meant 'continued along the Bacup Road', because he would have already been on the Bacup Road most of the way from Bacup. This error may have been his, or it may reflect a lack of care on the part of the police officer who took down his statement.

If Warwick was suggesting that what he had heard at 1 am that Sunday morning was Margaret disposing of the body, then he would be wrong. The body was not there when the transport men who were walking home had passed the house at **3.40 am,** but it was found at **3.55 am** by their colleagues travelling by bus, giving a fairly precise and narrow window of time during which it had been placed there. What he might have heard at 1 am, however, was Margaret going out to dispose of the hammer head and Nancy's shopping bag and handbag.

---

[33] This boy was Leon Vaessen, who would find fame as a professional footballer in the 1950s and 60s. He and his mother were evacuated to Lancashire during WW2 and billeted with Margaret Allen and her mother.

Cherchez l'homme

The statement made by Emily Whittaker, alleging she had seen Nancy out and about in the company of a man on the Saturday evening, was put to Nancy's good friend, Mrs Jordan. Mrs Jordan said she had never heard her friend mention the name of any man – save for one Dick Holden. Some years ago, according to Mrs Jordan, Holden, who had been courting Nancy for around six years, had suddenly dropped her to marry a Mrs Flaxer, a widow with a farm at Hall Carr. The couple had only been married for a few years when that lady died and Holden had sold up and gone to live at Haslingden, after which Holden and Nancy *'got pally again'*. Mrs Jordan alleged that Nancy *'was always going to his home'*.[34]

An alibi?

Margaret's sister, Mary Alice Peel, told police that Margaret had visited her again two days later, on Monday 30th August, and they had discussed the murder, which by now was the talk of the town. Mary Alice said Margaret had expressed concern as she had heard that Mary Alice had fainted. Mary Alice said the cause of her fainting was that she had heard a rumour – a premature rumour at that stage, as it turned out – that Margaret had been arrested for the murder. However, Margaret had reassured her that she had merely been interviewed briefly by police and had only been asked whether she had heard or seen anything. She told her sister, however, that she had been talking to reporters about the case.

Margaret told Mary Alice she didn't really know the victim and that she was just *'some old woman'*. Oddly, she now repaid the half-crown she had borrowed from Mary Alice on the Saturday. Either she had changed her mind about going to London, or, more likely, the story of the child's illness was a fabrication. Perhaps Margaret did not want to have money on her if and when the police re-interviewed her.

Given that, according to Mary Alice, Margaret nowadays only visited her sister every two or three months, Mary Alice thought it worth mentioning that Margaret had called to see her again just the following day, making three visits in the space of four days. That visit was at 12.30 on Tuesday 31 August. Mary Alice said she had gone out shopping, leaving Margaret alone in the house and Margaret was still there on her return fifteen minutes later. Margaret had left soon after 1pm, and it

---

[34] This may be untrue, however, as there appears to be no record of a marriage between parties named Flaxer and Holden in the registration records for England and Wales during Nancy Chadwick's lifetime.

seemed there had been no particular reason for the visit. One wonders why Margaret felt a sudden need to be near family members whom she usually visited infrequently.

Given all the sightings of Nancy Chadwick on the day of her death, which sightings range from 9.20 am up to 10.30 pm, and all of them seeming credible, it is difficult to identify a time frame within which she had met her death. If Dr Kay's estimate of time of death – between 6pm and 8pm – were accurate, then Margaret Allen had a solid alibi given by her sister and her nephew's wife, who put her in Bacup between the hours of 1.30 pm and 9 pm.

A witness disappears

The detectives next decided to re-interview Mary Alice Peel, perhaps to see whether they could break that alibi. Presumably, they were concerned about the disparity between the account of Margaret's whereabouts given by her relatives and the statement by Mary Ann Evans that Margaret was at home mending shoes that lunchtime up until 2.30 pm, as well as the conflicting statement by Fred Wilcock who said he had spoken to Margaret in Rawtenstall at 7.55 pm. Maybe it had crossed the detectives' minds that Mary Alice and Bridget might have given Margaret a false alibi.

When they arrived at Plantation Street in Bacup, however, to their surprise, the detectives found Mary Alice Peel and family had suddenly left the country. Mary Alice was quickly tracked down to the west of Ireland and, at Woodmansey's request, Irish police officers went to an address in County Mayo to interview her. However, Mary Alice declined to speak to them. Why Mary Alice went to Ireland was not established, but choosing to leave the country suddenly, when one's sister has just been arrested for murder, is surely a curious thing to do.

If Mary Alice's account of having fainted at the rumour of Margaret's arrest is actually true, this would suggest there was a bond between the sisters. At seven years Mary Alice's junior, and as the youngest surviving sibling, Margaret would have been the 'baby' of the family as the girls grew up. They had been separated and sent to different children's homes for a couple of years, but this unhappy experience may have brought them even closer together. Mary Alice, Margaret and their late mother had lived near to each other in Bacup for all but the past five years.

It is feasible, therefore, that the reason Margaret went to see Mary Alice three times in four days was to persuade her to provide a false alibi for the day of the murder. Mary Alice may have agreed to this and she may have gone along with this up to the point of Margaret's arrest, when she realised she would have to perjure herself in court, and so instead she chose to flee to Ireland.

It makes little sense, however, for Margaret to seek a false alibi for the afternoon and evening of 28 August, but then to tell police she had carried out the murder earlier that morning, at a time when she had no alibi. In fact, why confess at all if she had already gone to the trouble of arranging a false alibi? Was the confession indeed tricked or browbeaten out of her? Notwithstanding Dr Kay's estimate of time of death, was she coerced into stating she had carried out the murder during the hours for which she had no alibi? Or was it simply that Margaret was just not thinking clearly?

Did she not have the mental capacity to think her way out of trouble? Dr Cormack, the prison medical officer would later assess her as being *'of fair intelligence though not of high scholastic ability'*, so Margaret was not stupid. Might her cognitive processes have been temporarily affected, however, perhaps by anxiety or depression?

If Nancy had been killed later on the Saturday evening, as Dr Kay asserted, where had she been all day? Why had she not returned home at lunchtime, as she had promised her elderly employer she would? Had she perhaps run into the mysterious Dick Holden and decided to spend the day and evening with him, leaving poor Paddy Whittaker to fend for himself?

Had she gone to spend time with Holden at his Haslingden home, as Mrs Jordan claimed she was wont to do? Yet the only witness to see Nancy with a man had only seen them together late that evening. Other witnesses said they had seen Nancy around the town on her own at different times that day and during early evening. Assuming they were not all mistaken, it seems Nancy had plenty of opportunity to return home to give Paddy his lunch but, for some reason, had chosen not to.

Why so many discrepancies?

The many disparities regarding the time of death and the movements of both victim and killer remain unresolved. One former patient of Dr Kay would describe him as being 'too flippant'. Perhaps this flippancy suggests a superficial or less than serious approach to his work. It is certainly odd that his estimate of the time of death is so far out of accord with Margaret's estimate of when she had killed Nancy, and is at odds also with the statements of witnesses who saw Nancy alive after Dr Kay declares she was dead.

Does this raise doubt, therefore, that it was Margaret Allen who killed Nancy Chadwick? If not Margaret, then who else could have killed her? Could the man seen with Nancy at 1030 that night have been the killer? Of course, he was seen by only one witness, Emily Whittaker. Was that man Dick Holden? From Mrs Jordan's account of him, Holden, if he existed at all, sounds like something of a gold digger. Having allegedly acquired Mrs Flaxer's farm, he may also have been interested in Nancy's four properties, but to acquire these he would have to marry Nancy before even contemplating killing her.

The police did not try to find Holden, however, nor did they enquire into any other male acquaintances Nancy may have had. We do know that her nephew, William Barnes, said he had anticipated inheriting *'a little money'* from his aunt, albeit that, ultimately, she did not leave him anything in her will. It is not known – because he was not asked – whether he was actually aware that he was not mentioned in her will and whether, if he did know, he felt aggrieved about this. William was planning his wedding to his sweetheart, Hilda Raymond, for the following July, so an inheritance would have been welcome.

There is, of course, nothing to suggest Barnes was in any way involved in his aunt's death. In any case, Emily Whittaker estimated the man she had seen with Nancy was significantly older than 28-year-old William, albeit that she seemed to confuse 'elderly' with 'middle aged'. However, William Barnes was never actually asked to account for his whereabouts on the day of Nancy's death.

William was the illegitimate son of Nancy's half sister, Alice. Alice had died just six months before Nancy, in March 1948, in the infirmary at the Moorland Institute in Haslingden. This had been the workhouse where Margaret's father had died but, in 1948, it was a charitable hospital for the poor. This suggests that, unlike Nancy, Alice was not financially secure. Might William Barnes have resented this? Once again, this is pure speculation

Mrs Whittaker said the man she saw with Nancy had obviously been drinking. Might the brutal method of Nancy's death be the result of a drunken man's rage? It is possible. However, it seems that, once

Margaret Allen had confessed, so certain of her guilt were they, the police did not consider any alternative suspects.

Turning to Margaret's confession, so readily given but so short on detail, it is hard to imagine why anyone in their right mind would confess to a crime if they had not committed it, but was Margaret Allen in her right mind? Whether guilty or not, why would she confess so easily when she had so much to lose?

Was Margaret coerced into confessing? Or, might this lonely, confused woman, one of the youngest of an excessively large brood of children, the child of an oft-absent father and a loving but impoverished mother, have wanted to be – for the first time in her life – the centre of attention?

Detectives Woodmansey and Stevens give the crime scene their full attention.
(image courtesy of Peter Fisher)

Chapter 9 – The Plea

'Commiserate with an unstable woman passing through the change of life; an abnormal woman who had declared that an operation had made her into a man; an unbalanced woman who had committed a purposeless, fatuous and mad murder' – Margaret's defence counsel.

Since 1843, the M'Naghten rules have applied in English law. These rules hold that every man is to be presumed to be sane and to possess a sufficient degree of reason to be responsible for his crimes, unless and until the contrary be proved to a court's satisfaction. The rules also hold that, to establish a defence on the grounds of insanity, it must be clearly proven that, at the time of committing the act, the accused was labouring under such a defect of reason – from disease of the mind – as not to know the nature and quality of the act he was doing; or, if he did know it, that he did not know what he was doing was wrong.

Just across the English Channel, however, the law is applied a little differently. Whereas the British system is 'adversarial', meaning the case is usually won by whoever has the most competent advocate, the French system, modelled upon the Code of Napoleon, is 'inquisitorial' – that is, a judge is appointed with the power to interview all parties personally and is compelled to look at all the evidence to try to glean the truth.

The French system, and those of certain other European countries, also accepts the concept of the *crime passionel*, a killing

94

carried out in the heat of a sudden rage and without pre-meditation. The nearest that British law comes to this definition is in considering whether an intolerable degree of provocation may mitigate such an unplanned act of killing. However, since Margaret did not claim she had been subjected to any particular provocation by Nancy Chadwick, but simply said she had felt 'irritated' by her, provocation was not put forward as the basis of her plea. Instead, her legal team opted for a plea of 'temporary insanity'.

Mens Rea

In the common law of England and many other countries, the standard test of criminal liability is encompassed in the Latin phrase *'actus reus non facit reum nisi mens sit rea'* – the act is not culpable unless the mind is guilty. The phrase *'mens rea'* – literally, 'guilty mind' – refers to the mental state of the perpetrator of a criminal act at the time that act was committed. It invites consideration of whether or not that perpetrator's mental state was sufficiently sane to render them culpable.

So, did Margaret Allen harbour guilty intent when she attacked Nancy Chadwick? Was she wholly in her right mind and therefore legally culpable, or, at that moment, was she subject to some abnormal state of mind? Was she, as her counsel would claim, gripped by some form of temporary insanity?

Usually, it is only when someone's behaviour veers away from the normal that concern is aroused for their sanity, but what is 'normal' behaviour? The line between eccentric behaviour and abnormal behaviour is a fine one and a subjective one, and therefore the difference is sometimes difficult to assess or to prove.

As we will see, Margaret did exhibit some odd behaviour, both before and after the murder. However, her defence team were unaware of this. Unfortunately, she did not provide her counsel with sufficient knowledge of her situation to fully support a plea of 'temporary insanity'.

Her counsel knew nothing of the problems caused by her gender predicament. He knew she had allowed herself to fall deeper and deeper into debt but he did not know she actually had money in the bank to cover most of that debt. Her counsel did not know of her neglected home and her inability to care for herself, though he did know of her suicide attempt because Annie would refer to this in her testimony in court. Why did Margaret not open up about all this? Had he known, could her counsel perhaps have made more of this?

95

In the 1940s mental illness was far from being an unknown occurrence. The debt and deprivation of the hungry 'thirties had led many people to breakdowns and suicide, and the effects of stress on the combatants and civilian population following World War Two were equally obvious. However, throughout the twentieth century, mental illness still carried a major stigma. Margaret already had to bear the stigmas of illegitimacy and gender dysphoria. Perhaps she did not wish also to be labelled insane.

Mens sana?

Assuming Margaret did commit this sudden and savage murder, was she wholly sane when she did so? Well, Margaret's behaviour around the time of the murder was certainly bizarre.

33-year-old Thomas Glenavon Edmondson was one of the police constables keeping guard at the scene following the discovery of Nancy's body. After the body had been removed from the street, Edmondson had spotted Margaret standing in her doorway and he asked her if she knew who the dead woman was. Margaret replied that it might be a woman named 'Chaddock' who often passed by.

Unbelievably, Margaret then accompanied Edmondson to the mortuary to view the body. It is not recorded whether this was at his request or whether she volunteered to do so. In his statement Edmondson says:

'She peered down at the face and said she wasn't sure but was sure the coat was the same. She moved her hands over the dead woman's face and asked if she could open the mouth, as Chaddock had 'two fangs'. I wouldn't let her.'

One might expect a killer to flee the scene of the murder, maintain a low profile and avoid speaking to the police, but apparently not all killers do so. Perverse though it seems, some murderers are drawn back to the crime scene, and may even enjoy watching the investigation unfold. Some even seek to insinuate themselves into the investigation.

Psychologists suggest a number of reasons why this may be so. In the case of a 'spree' killer or serial killer, it may be a kind of psychopathic urge which leaves the perpetrator obsessed and thrilled by what he has done and wanting to re-live the excitement of the act. An extreme egotist, who has enjoyed exercising the power of life and death,

96

may be arrogant enough to enjoy watching the police failing in their efforts to catch him. However, Margaret seems to have been neither a spree or serial killer nor an extreme egotist.

Most of the reasons psychologists suggest for this type of attention-seeking behaviour are connected with a defect of mind or personality. Logically, therefore, one would expect wholly sane killers to distance themselves from the crime scene and to disassociate themselves from the victim.

Margaret Allen, however, was not behaving logically. She was actively drawing attention to herself. She could hardly avoid the place where the body was found, of course, since she lived just feet away, but, having committed such a brutal and repulsive act, it seems incredible that she would want to view and even to touch the corpse. Oddly, however, she did not appear constrained by more 'normal' feelings of revulsion or remorse.

More strange behaviour

Some press reports alleged Margaret had boasted to reporters that she had been the last person to see Nancy Chadwick alive. Did she really say this? Logically, the last person to have seen Nancy alive would have been the killer. Did this logic not occur to Margaret, or, in this respect also, was she simply not behaving logically?

Margaret's sister, Mary Alice Peel, would tell the police that Margaret had admitted she had been speaking with the press, although Mary Alice did not say what Margaret had actually said to the reporters. This comment stands out as a non-sequitur in the alibi Mary Alice was providing for her sister, and is clearly unhelpful to Margaret's case. Like many of the other statements recorded by the police in this case, it is disjointed and reads like an answer to a direct question put by the police, rather than as a spontaneous narrative.

It is possible the police had read Margaret's comment in the press and, since it supported their contention that Margaret was the killer, they tried to add credibility to it by getting Mary Alice to confirm it. Alternatively, the police may even have fed Margaret's alleged comment to the press in the first place.

If Margaret had indeed made such a comment to reporters, however, it was a remarkably stupid thing for a seemingly intelligent person to do. 'Intelligent' is how the prison Medical Officer would later describe Margaret. In speaking to the press and trying to insert herself into the limelight in this way, rather than lying low, she seemed to lack any sense of self-preservation. It was almost as if she wished to be caught. By anyone's standards, this surely cannot constitute normal behaviour.

Another witness, Jack Ives, tried to suggest she had done something even more foolish to incriminate herself:

'At 3 pm on Sunday 29 August, I saw Margaret Allen, whom I know, in Fall Barn Fold. At the level crossing, we saw something on the stones. The Police were told and they retrieved it. Then, Maggie pointed to something else in the river. The policeman got it and it was the [dead] *woman's bag.'*

However, Ives' testimony is firmly contradicted by that of another witness. Gertrude Cain of 15 Fall Barn Fold deposed:

'I was standing with Margaret Allen and a man I did not know when items were found in the river, but it was me who spotted the string bag in the brook.'

Unfortunately, Jack Ives' incorrect and dangerously damning statement was the one which would be read out in court by the prosecution counsel as part of his opening address, and it was Ives' comment, not Gertrude Cain's correction, which was reported in the press and which would be repeated in subsequent accounts of the case over the years.

The defence counsel was unable to refute Ives' assertion because, like so much of the witness testimony, Gertrude Cain's statement was never disclosed to him.

Margaret's delusions

Other aspects of Margaret Allen's odd behaviour during the weeks prior to the murder were attested to by another witness. Bacup grocer Douglas McLeod Walton gave a deposition regarding several visits made to his shop in July and August 1948 by Margaret, whom he knew from when she had lived in that town. He said she had made purchases in his shop on 24 July and he had noticed she had four or five one-pound notes in her pocket[35]. She had told him she was going to Blackpool the following day with her friend, Annie Tattersall[36].

Walton said Margaret returned to his shop the following Friday, 30 July, and said she had indeed been to Blackpool. However, Annie would recount to police only one Blackpool trip and that had been a couple of months earlier in May 1948. Allegedly, Margaret then said a number of things to Walton which he said he took to be just 'stories'. She said she would be going into a convalescent home in Grange-over-Sands. She also told him a brother of hers had died and had left her £500[37] and two houses.

Then she returned to the shop again on 6 August and claimed she had won £825[38] on the football pools, of which she had deposited £300 in the Post Office and £500 with the Burnley Building Society. Oddly, however, she then asked Mr Walton to lend her £12[39] with which to buy clothes to visit her solicitor's office. Walton claimed he had lent her this money, but said that, the following day, Margaret was back asking for a further loan.

If this were true, to have lent Margaret such a large sum was extraordinarily generous of Walton, especially as, although he may have known her since childhood, she had not lived in Bacup for some years and so is unlikely to have been a regular customer of late. Perhaps, like Beatrice Haworth's daughter who, allegedly, had lent her two shillings, he found Margaret a particularly sympathetic and likeable character.

The police may have considered Walton's information to be of value, suggesting as it does that Margaret was expecting to come into money, perhaps dishonestly. Accordingly, his testimony was admitted into evidence. A murder conviction is always easier to achieve if pre-meditation can be demonstrated. Clearly, the large sums of money Margaret claimed to have acquired were just fantasy, though Walton suggests she had £5 on her at a time when she had mounting debts and was under threat of eviction.

Surely, any sane person would have tried to reduce their debts rather than borrowing and incurring further expense on clothes and

---

[35] £5 represented almost three weeks' worth of Margaret's benefit payments.

[36] Annie Cook, neé Tattersall, seems to have reverted to her maiden name around that time.

[37] Worth over £12,000 at today's values.

[38] Almost £21,000 today.

[39] Worth over £300 today.

holidays? Margaret still had her untouched savings of £32 in the Trustees Savings Bank, which sum could have gone a long way to fending off her creditors and the bailiffs. Instead, she had taken the desperate step of selling her cooker for £9 but had then blown the money on a holiday in Blackpool with Annie. Though Margaret's debts would be mentioned in court, her bank balance, however, was not.

Does such financial recklessness sit within the parameters of normal behaviour? Spinning Mr Walton such yarns was yet another way in which Margaret, already the object of local curiosity for her habit of dressing as a man, drew attention to herself in the weeks before the murder. Perhaps the best judge of Margaret Allen, however, is the person who knew her best, her only friend Annie Cook.

Annie would testify that she saw Margaret from 1030 am on Saturday 28th August continuously throughout the morning, with just a twenty-minute absence, until noon, then met her again briefly at around 1.40. More of Margaret's peculiarities are revealed in the statement Annie gave to detectives, as is the intrusive line of questioning those detectives now pursued:

'Statement of Annie Cook, age 32 years, cone winder, of 15 Union Terrace, Rawtenstall. I am the wife of WILLIE COOK, from whom I am living apart by mutual consent. He lives at 14 Sutcliffe St., Britannia, Bacup. I am employed at Victoria works, Cloughfold.

I've been friendly with Margaret Allen about 2 years and having been going out with her regularly. I have slept at her house on about 3 occasions in Jan and Feb 1948. We slept together. The last time I slept with her she had pyjamas on and I had a nightgown on. She said to me 'we have been going out long enough now together. Can't we start having connections?' I told her 'No. I am parted from my husband and don't want to bother.' That was all that was said. As far as I know, I don't know what she was going to have connections with, from her point of view. I have never seen her in the nude.

She has told me on many occasions that she was father to a child of a woman evacuee that used to stay with her. If we went anywhere together, she used to say 'don't call me Maggie. Call me Bill'.

We went to Blackpool during Whit week 1948 and she used the men's lavatories there. I have never known her dress as a woman. I have known her to smoke a pipe at home and at Burnley Victoria Palace Theatre on about 3 occasions during the year. She always smokes cigarettes and drinks beer from a pint glass. She doesn't owe me money and I don't owe her any. I generally saw her every night and she never mentioned the name of Mrs Chadwick to me.

On Saturday 28 August, I was not working. I had arranged to see her at her house in Bacup Road that morning at 10 o'clock to show her my divorce papers. I had some errands to do for my mother and it was about 10.25 am when I met her coming along Alma Cottages towards me. She turned back and we went to the Food Office. On the way, we went over the crossing along Fall Barn to Bacup Rd where she called in at her house. I didn't go in. She was in the house about 20 minutes.

After we'd been in the Food Office on Lord Street, we went to Melia's in Bank St. Then she asked if I was going to the 'Tup' [Ram's Head hotel] for a drink. I told her it wasn't the time to be going for a drink but she said she could get in anytime. I suggested we should go to Ashworth Arms at Cloughfold. We went by way of Kay St and Bacup road and arrived at 11.30. She ordered a glass of mild for herself and a Guinness for me. We were sat in the best room and she kept laughing and sort of staring at me. I asked why but she did not reply. That was the only unusual thing.

We stopped there till a quarter to twelve and then came down the Bacup Road as far as Cawl Co-op shop. We stopped there talking for a few moments and I arranged to see her at 5pm at her house. At about twenty to two, she called at my house. She said she was going on a bit of business about a new mackintosh. She didn't say where and left. I did not see her again until I saw her in the court at Rawtenstall this morning. She never mentioned the name of Chadwick.'

When they had interviewed Margaret, detectives had not queried her habit of cross-dressing. One wonders why, then, when they interviewed Annie, the issue of Margaret's dress and sexuality suddenly became relevant, as is clear from the statement above. Perhaps they were trying to get Annie to incriminate herself.

If the police could establish that there had been a sexual relationship between the women, they might be able to infer from that intimacy that Annie must have had prior knowledge of, or even been involved in Nancy's murder. Or perhaps it was simply the detectives' intention to present a less savoury side of Margaret's character to the jury in hopes of securing a conviction.

Annie's statement does not seem wholly helpful to Margaret. Margaret's laughing and staring whilst in the pub a few hours after the murder might suggest she was keeping some sort of guilty secret. One wonders why Annie felt she needed to say this at all. As with Mary Alice Peel's statement, however, this does not seem to be a spontaneous narrative. Each part of the statement reads as an answer to a question. Annie was not well educated and, unlike Margaret, has never been described as being intelligent. If the detectives had exerted Capstick-like interrogation techniques upon her, it would not have been too difficult for them to steer and manipulate her answers.

As to the issue of Margaret's gender anomaly, this was never fully explored by Margaret's GP or by the Prison Medical Officer, mainly because she failed to tell *them* the real reason behind her choice of masculine apparel. Moreover, she maintained she was a heterosexual female who dressed as a man purely for convenience.

This stance would make even less sense when Margaret elected to appear at her trial dressed as a man. One wonders what the court made of Annie's statements regarding Margaret's request for 'connections'. In the absence of any clarification by Margaret herself, doubtless they inferred that Margaret was a lesbian. Margaret would say nothing to disabuse them of this notion.

Of course, Margaret seems to have been given to making fantastical claims on occasion. Telling the gullible grocer she had come into money was presumably a ploy to persuade him she was good risk for a loan. Yet, as her bank balance reflects, she did not need a loan.

She had also tried to convince people that the surgery she had undergone in 1930 was sex-change surgery, yet her medical records show this to be untrue. Though she had not repeated this claim to her GP or to the prison medical officer, it came out during the examination of Annie Cook, and the defence counsel would refer to it in his final submission.

Margaret had even tried to persuade Annie she had fathered the child evacuee. This, too, was demonstrably untrue. Little Leon Vaessen was born in London in 1940 *before* he and his mother Charlotte came to lodge with Margaret. The child's birth registration confirms his biological father was a Dutch national also named Leon Vaessen. Margaret's family and her neighbours in Bacup would have known Margaret could not be the child's parent. So, was Margaret trying to delude others, or was she self-delusional?

Margaret's mental health

Given Margaret's erratic and deprived upbringing, it would be surprising if her health, both physical and mental, had not suffered from time to time. The array of physical ailments to which she was prone may have been caused by her mental state. Alternatively, they may simply have been a bid for attention.

Tellingly, the instances when she was caught stealing did not occur when she was unemployed or in debt, but rather at times when she was in full time work and enjoying a steady, if modest, income. It is possible these incidents, too, represented attention-seeking or a cry for help.

Of course, Margaret did have good reason to be depressed. Having long been the breadwinner in her relationship with her mother, Margaret had cut her familial ties to Bacup following her mother's death and had moved into the old police lockup at Rawtenstall where, probably for the first time in her life, she had lived all alone. Living there may have been more convenient for her, given that her employment then was in Rawtenstall, but she had found herself alone and friendless.

Without her mother's influence and help, she had also found herself unable to keep either her person or her household in good order. Several years of 'invisible' illnesses and visits to her GP had followed. From 1946 she had gradually fallen deeper and deeper into debt, and then she had been unemployed for almost all of 1948. These, surely, were factors sufficient to depress anyone.

In 1948, the most commonly applied treatment for depression was electro convulsive therapy, or 'electric shock treatment' as it was commonly termed. Various accounts suggest this treatment was also administered to some patients as a possible 'cure' for homosexuality and other sexual 'aberrations'. There is nothing in Margaret's GP's records to suggest she was subjected to ECT, but then her medical files do not include any definitive account of her treatment during her prolonged hospital stays, so it is just possible that she did undergo ECT.

Back then, before the introduction of anti-spasmodic drugs, ECT was a most uncomfortable experience causing patients to convulse violently, and so injuries to neck or spine and severe headaches were unfortunate but common side effects. The treatment did, and still does, provide many patients with relief from depression, although many have reported that this was because it causes a degree of amnesia, making them forget, for a time at least, what had caused their depression in the first place. Short term memory loss was an unfortunate side effect of the treatment.

If Margaret's GP had failed to diagnose depression, then the hospital doctors may not have identified it either. If Margaret had been subjected to ECT, however, – albeit that there is no evidence to suggest that she was – she might have been unable, rather than unwilling, to recall events leading up to the murder. Like so much in her case, however, this would be pure conjecture.

The prison MO found her memory of her past history to be satisfactory, yet he made no mention of the quality of her short-term memory. He did not find it unsatisfactory that she would not, or could not recall more detail of her motive for killing or of events leading up to the murder she had so recently committed.

Annie would later recount to Huggett and Berry that Margaret had frequently complained to her of headaches and would often sit, head in hands, crying because of these headaches. It is odd, then, that headaches do not feature amongst the many complaints she took to her GP. Did she not tell him of these, or did he simply not record them in her notes? Was this because it was accepted they were side effects of treatment she had undergone? Or perhaps she invented the headaches simply to attract sympathy. Perhaps the headaches, like her suicide attempt, also represented a cry for help.

Annie's statement to the police reflects the fact that Margaret's feelings for her included a desire for sexual contact, though Annie suggests that, for her part, those particular feelings were not reciprocated. Though the two women were undeniably close, Annie's alleged refusal to take their relationship to a physical level, if that be true, must have been a disappointment to someone like Margaret who struggled daily to assert her gender. What surer way, perhaps, of asserting one's gender than engaging in a sexual relationship?

Huggett and Berry's interview with Annie led them to conclude that this was Margaret's first experience of romantic love. This love had come to Margaret in middle age, at a time when her loss of youth and a diminishing opportunity for romance was now made all too apparent by the onset of the menopause.

As the prison MO would state, typical symptoms of the aptly-named 'change of life' include anxiety, irritability, agitation and restlessness. Margaret certainly owned up to and demonstrated these symptoms. Her anxiety that she might lose Annie had even provoked an attempt to kill herself. Had it been that same anxiety which had driven this agitated and irritable menopausal woman to kill someone else?

In their book, Huggett and Berry draw a comparison with the 1886 trial of one Mrs Taylor, a grocer's wife who, having borne eleven children in the space of seventeen years, and finding herself menopausal and overly anxious about debt, cut the throats of three of her children. Mrs Taylor immediately confessed and could give no reason or excuse for what she had done. The jury took due account of her menopausal state and, accepting that her mind had been unbalanced at the time of the murders, returned a verdict of 'guilty but insane', so she was spared the rope.

Margaret's defence counsel might have had this case in mind when he opted to plead that Margaret, too, had acted under the effects of 'temporary insanity'. Sixty-two years after the acquittal of Mrs Taylor, however, the jury in the case of Margaret Allen would not be so understanding. Like the unfortunate Mrs Taylor, Margaret had made little attempt to conceal her crime. One would have expected even someone who was as poor a housekeeper as Margaret to have made a little more of an effort to clean up after wilfully committing a murder, yet one small damp rag indicated Margaret's very half-hearted attempt to mop up the bloodstains. Also like Mrs Taylor, Margaret readily confessed to what she had done, yet had no explanation for it.

Why did Margaret confess so readily? Was she coerced into confessing? Or, if her confession was entirely voluntary, could she really have doubted for a single moment that she would hang?

The Prospect of Execution

Foolish though her prompt confession may seem, Margaret may at least have had good cause to expect she would not be executed. In April 1948, the House of Commons had voted, by a majority of 245 votes to 222, to amend the Criminal Justice Bill and to suspend the death penalty for a trial period of five years. Following this vote, all convicted and condemned criminals were automatically reprieved. This reprieve was even extended to Donald Thomas, who had shot a policeman three times and had then cruelly delivered the final *coup de grâce* as that policeman lay dying at his feet.

There were twenty-six such reprieves and no executions between March and October of 1948. It was during that moratorium, on 1st September, that Margaret had confessed and was arrested. Given that the

House of Commons had voted in 1948 for a *five-year* suspension of capital punishment, even as she awaited her trial, Margaret would have had legitimate expectation of avoiding the hangman's noose.

Unfortunately for Margaret, the House of Lords soon overturned the Commons' vote and the five-year suspension was prematurely curtailed. Executions resumed on 18 November 1948 with the hanging of Stanley Clarke. Peter Griffiths, the afore-mentioned child killer from Blackburn, was executed the following day.

As the date of Margaret's December trial loomed, the chances of her being handed down a custodial, rather than a death sentence, now seemed increasingly slight. However, Margaret's defence team still entertained a degree of hope, by virtue of the fact that it had been twelve years since a woman had been executed in the UK. Perhaps all Margaret had to do was convince a judge and jury that she *was* a woman.

Chapter 10 – The Trial

'I don't think Allen ever realised the seriousness of her position,' –
Kenneth Yates, Margaret's solicitor.

After several remand hearings held in Rawtenstall County Court,
the trial of Margaret Allen was held at Manchester Assize Courts on 8
December 1948. The Assizes comprised a massive and forbidding Gothic
building which had been very badly bomb-damaged during the
Manchester Blitz. The building was not looking at its dignified best,
being shoddily shorn up whilst awaiting demolition. Nevertheless,
standing in the dock in that cavernous courtroom must have been a most
intimidating experience for Margaret.

Having been granted legal aid, she was represented by Kenneth
Yates, aged thirty-two, of the Haslingden firm Robert Arthur Cotton
Solicitors. This seems to have been Yates' first (and seemingly only ever)
murder case, but he seems to have done his best for Margaret, despite her
reluctance or inability to give a plausible reason for killing Nancy
Chadwick. Yates may have been relatively inexperienced in the field of
murder, but the same could not be said for Margaret's barrister.

William Gorman KC was appointed as Margaret's defence
counsel. Gorman was a 58-year-old bachelor, who had been made a judge
in 1934 and had served as Recorder for both Wigan and Liverpool. A
politically active member of the Liberal Party, he had several times stood
(unsuccessfully) in local elections. As the son of a Wigan shopkeeper and

107

grandson of an Irish immigrant, he seemed empathetically suited to representing working class Irishman's daughter Margaret Allen.

With several murder trials under his belt, Gorman would be knighted in 1950 and, in 1962, would preside over the A6 Murder Case – the longest murder trial in British history. Margaret Allen's 1948 trial, however, would be the shortest trial of any of the fifteen women executed for murder during the twentieth century.

Manchester Assize Courts at the end of the war and as they would appear when Margaret's trial was held. The tower on the extreme right of the picture, and the lower round tower to the left of that, are part of Strangeways Prison, in which Margaret was held and where she would be executed. (Source unattributable).

The judge presiding over the trial was 54-year-old Lord Justice Frederick Aked Sellers, another unsuccessful Liberal politician. Disappointingly, the proceedings did not receive the sort of intense press coverage given to most twentieth century murder cases.

Newspapers mainly reported the opening address of prosecuting counsel Mr. (Albert) Denis Gerrard KC, including his inaccurate assertion regarding the accused having pointed out the deceased's bag in the river. Gerrard emphasised robbery as the most likely motive for the murder, even though no evidence would be presented to suggest that Margaret had relieved old Nancy of any money whatsoever.

Margaret wore her best (man's) suit, shirt, tie and brogues as she sat in the dock. Perhaps because of her odd and off-putting appearance as much as her lack of satisfactory explanation for her crime, Gorman decided not to call her to give evidence in her own defence. He may have felt she would not be able to evince the court's sympathy. In this, he was probably right.

The written statement Margaret had made to the police, maintaining she had been irritated by Nancy and had been *'in one of my funny moods'* when she had savagely beaten her to death, was read aloud to the court. This statement probably sounded brief, cold-blooded and unremorseful, especially when read out by the prosecutor, but, since she did not take the stand herself, Margaret had no opportunity to make a better impression, to explain her motives or to express remorse and regret.

Margaret passed her 42nd birthday in a cell at Strangeways prison, presumably without celebration. Although, since her death, many who had known and worked with Margaret would comment on her kindness and the consideration she showed toward others, not a single person came forward to act as a character witness at her trial. Even Annie was designated by the police as a prosecution witness.

Disclosure of evidence

Nowadays, police and prosecution counsel are under legal obligation to disclose to the defence team and to the court *all* the evidence gathered in an investigation, even that evidence which might be unhelpful to the prosecution's case. However, that was not the situation in 1948.

The police files show that none of the testimony of those witnesses who claimed to have seen Nancy Chadwick alive after 9.30 am on the day of her murder was presented at the trial. Perhaps the most critical omission was that of the statements of Fred Taylor and his daughter Nellie Parry, which belied Margaret's account of the time of death but, equally importantly, offered a more credible and perhaps mitigating motive for her killing of Nancy Chadwick. Also withheld was the albeit dubious 'alibi' given by Margaret's sister Mary Alice and her daughter-in-law Bridget, who did not, in any case, show up for Margaret's trial.

Medical evidence

Dr Kay's initial estimate of the time of death, which conflicted with Margaret's confession, was not presented either. Instead, the medical evidence focused on the testimony of the surgeon who had conducted the post-mortem and who described the savagery of the injuries – he now described 'ten or more' blows administered by a heavy instrument – which had caused Nancy Chadwick's ageing skull to cave in.

Although Mr Gorman would rely on a defence strategy of 'temporary insanity', there was no witness testimony to support this. No-one took the stand to give evidence as to any quirk of Margaret's character or behaviour which might confirm her counsel's contention that the balance of her mind had been disturbed at the time of the killing. No independent medical professional was called in to interpret her GP's records or to comment on the likelihood that she was suffering from depression or any other kind of mental disturbance.

Only the conclusions of the prison MO, Dr. Cormack – based on, we know not how many, or how few interviews with Margaret – were presented. He repeated that Margaret had been well behaved in prison, apart from exhibiting what he considered to be, given her situation, *an understandable degree of anxiety and emotion'*. He was not challenged about the means by which he reached his conclusion that the anxiety and emotion she displayed had only arisen after her arrest and was not present before the murder. He told the court that Margaret had described to him how she had felt dizzy and irritable immediately prior to Nancy entering her house, but he drew no further conclusion from this, and nor did the defence counsel seek to exploit this to Margaret's advantage.

Cormack continued to maintain that, whilst in prison, Margaret had *'manifested no signs of mental illness, disorder or defect'*. He repeated his conclusion that:

'the accused is at present passing through the menopause. During this phase, women may be subject to many and varied symptoms, including vertigo, irritability and emotional disturbances. I think there is little doubt the dizzy bouts are secondary to menopausal changes. After careful review of all the facts of the case known to me, I am of the opinion that the accused, at the time of the committing of the act, was not suffering from such a defect of reason from disease of the mind* as not to know the nature and quality of the act or that what she was doing was wrong'.

*Here, Cormack was interpreting the M'Naghten Rules, which specify that the only type of *'defect of reason'* which might render the killer not culpable was that which results from *'disease of the mind'*. In Margaret's case, however, no disease of the mind had been diagnosed by Cormack or by anyone else.

Cormack commented on how clean and well-behaved she had been when brought before him. Of course, he had only seen her after her arrest, in the pristine and well-ordered confines of the prison. He had not observed her before the murder. Nor had he seen the chaotic home circumstances where, for the past year, she had been sitting around, lethargically weeping and complaining of headaches, as she had descended deeper and deeper into needless debt. He did not know she had funds in the bank with which she could have settled most of that debt. He had observed neither her self-neglect nor the semi-derelict and lice-infested environment in which she lived and where the murder had occurred.

Though he had not examined the medical records of any other family member, nevertheless, Cormack felt able to state with confidence that there was no history of mental illness in Margaret's family. The defence team did not have any independent medical specialist examine Margaret, and no independent expert witness was called to comment on her behaviour before or after the act in order to counter, or at least to balance Cormack's opinion.

The information Annie would later give to Huggett and Berry regarding Margaret's claimed headaches was not raised in court. This was probably because Annie was not asked, either at interview or in court, about her friend's state of mind. This would not have seemed relevant to the police, whose case was entirely based on robbery as a motive.

In his summation, Margaret's defence counsel invited the jury to

'commiserate with an unstable woman passing through the change of life; an abnormal woman who had declared that an operation had made her into a man; an unbalanced woman who had committed a purposeless, fatuous and mad murder'.

'Commiserate' seems such an inadequate word when pleading for someone's life. Perhaps, though, since Margaret either would not or could not give a satisfactory explanation for the murder, her counsel felt

111

he had too little information to work with. Perhaps he himself found it hard to do more than commiserate.

The judge, in summing up, was more assertive. Justice Sellers told the jury that, although the defence had invited them to bring in a verdict of 'guilty but insane', he did not think there was any evidence *'such as the law required'* to bring in such a verdict. There might well have been sufficient evidence to support such a verdict, however, had *all* the available evidence been put before the court.

In contrast to the later and better publicised Cameo Murder trial (1950), in which Margaret's counsel would appear for the prosecution, and in which the summing up alone would take six hours, Margaret Allen's entire trial lasted just five hours. Moreover, the jury of nine men and three women spent less than fifteen minutes deliberating on Margaret's crime before returning a verdict of 'guilty'. Asked if they wished to make any recommendation to mercy, the jury members declined to do so.

The defence strategy

Was the plea of 'temporary insanity' the best strategy Gorman could have adopted? Since the contradictory witness statements were not made available to him – statements which might have damaged the prosecution case, and might even have suggested an alternative killer – and given Margaret's bald and unrepentant confession, Gorman could hardly have entertained a 'not guilty' plea. Indeed, the strongest evidence against Margaret remained her own confession.

The physical evidence, however, most importantly the bloodstains in Margaret's house and on her clothing, was not conclusive proof of her guilt. The similarity of hair and fibres found at the scene to those found on the body was arguably coincidental, as was the proximity to Margaret's house of the body dump site and bloody drag marks.

However, had Gorman or Yates been permitted to see the statements of Fred Taylor and Nellie Parry in particular, which suggested there had been some sort of altercation between Margaret and Nancy earlier that morning, and had they been aware that the police had failed to follow up Mrs Whittaker's and Mrs Jordan's account of Nancy's alleged man friend, the defence team might have been able to explore and exploit these facts and might have followed an altogether different strategy.

If the defence team had been aware of that alleged exchange between Margaret and Nancy, during which Nancy had *'bit her damned head off'* and which had led Margaret to conclude *'the old bugger's crackers'*, Gorman might have opted instead for a defence based on Nancy having provoked Margaret.

Had Margaret not volunteered the feeble story about offering to obtain sugar for Nancy, and had she instead told Gorman what she had told Fred Taylor – that she had gone to see Nancy about the exchange of a house but Nancy had had bitten her head off – Gorman might have been able to coax more details of this from Margaret and might have been able to use this to her advantage.

The deceased's nephew had already described his aunt to the coroner's court as being 'abnormal'. However, it was not Nancy's abnormality which was on trial but Margaret's. It was Margaret's 'abnormality', described by her counsel as 'temporary insanity', which formed the basis of Gorman's plea for mercy. Had the full picture of Margaret's personal circumstances been known to the defence – and the fact that it was not was as much due to Margaret's reticence as to the police's cherry picking of evidence – might her plea have been different and might it have been successful?

The benefit of hindsight and foresight

What we nowadays understand about the experiences of transgendered individuals, as we now refer to them, is that they have long been subjected to harassment and stigmatisation. Psychologists say that this, added to their own sense of not belonging to an established gender culture, can typically lead to secrecy, self-denial, isolation and depression. The psychologists also say that transgendered individuals are more likely to have suicidal thoughts than is the general population.

Margaret's medical records revealed she had, at least once, been on the receiving end of a black eye, suggesting she was no stranger to the sort of physical abuse which cross-dressing did, and still does attract. Verbal abuse is likely to have been an even more common occurrence for Margaret. However, the stress this would undoubtedly have caused her was not something explored by her defence team.

Armed with more information about Margaret's life and a little understanding of her situation, Gorman might have sought to present to the jury a different aspect of her interaction with Nancy, and might have successfully argued extreme provocation as a motive or mitigating factor.

113

Would that, though, have been any more successful as a defence strategy? Well, later events would suggest that it could have been.

Six years later, on the other side of the Pennines in the Yorkshire city of Leeds, 40-year-old Sarah Lloyd would brutally murder her 86-year-old neighbour Edith Emsley. A long-standing falling-out had existed between the two women until, one day in 1955, Lloyd would enter her elderly neighbour's home and batter her to death with a spade. For good measure, she would pour a pan of boiling vegetables over the dead or dying woman before calmly taking herself and her daughter off to enjoy a film at the cinema.

Sarah Lloyd's counsel would venture a plea of provocation and, although Lloyd would be convicted of murder and sentenced to hang, she was to be reprieved two days before the sentence was due to be carried out and she would serve just seven years for the killing.

There was to be no great public outcry at either the killing of Emsley or at Lloyd's death sentence, or even at the reprieve, but nor would any petition be raised on Lloyd's behalf. Her husband's would be the lone voice pleading for clemency, and yet clemency was granted.

The difference between this case and Margaret Allen's is the nature of Lloyd's plea – provocation. There was also the fact that, unlike Margaret, Lloyd was not considered to be 'abnormal'. As a wife and mother, Sarah Lloyd would not display any sexual proclivities which a jury might find unacceptable. This, perhaps, is why she would be considered deserving of mercy whilst Margaret was not.

In 1955, whilst Sarah Lloyd languished in prison under sentence of death, another woman would also be sitting in a death cell awaiting execution. Ruth Ellis's death sentence would attract a petition of fifty thousand signatures, yet, unlike Lloyd, Ellis would hang. As a nightclub hostess who shot and killed the playboy boyfriend who had earlier beaten her and caused her to miscarry her child and had taken up with another woman, Ruth would attract the sympathy of the nation, but would attract neither the mercy of the court nor the clemency of the Home Secretary.

Like Sarah Lloyd, Ellis would opt for provocation as a defence. Unlike either Allen or Lloyd, however, Ellis would not be able to claim her crime was unpre-meditated, since she had used a gun to carry it out. Like Margaret, though, she would surrender to justice immediately and admit her crime. Like Margaret, she would not seek to mitigate her crime or to defend herself. Therefore, like Margaret, she was hanged. Perhaps, also like Margaret, she was hanged for what she was, just as much as for what she had done.

Margaret Allen would say nothing in her own defence. In fact, Margaret would say nothing at all. Therefore, Lord Justice Sellers had little option but to pronounce sentence of death by hanging.

Chapter 11 – The Appeals

'We, the undersigned, knew Margaret Allen and are aware of her peculiarities and respectfully request a reprieve to be granted' – plea by 163 Rawtenstall petitioners.

The announcement of Margaret's sentencing was reported in the evening's newspapers on the day of the trial, though it was not given the prominence which such news usually attracted. The story ranked surprisingly low even in the local Lancashire press.

One local paper printed it below the National Union of Boot and Shoe Operatives' announcement that footwear production had increased by sixteen percent over the pre-war levels, despite the industry having 13,000 fewer operatives than before the war. Well, the industry was about to lose one of its former operatives to judicial execution, yet the brief report on her conviction, sited much further down the page, said simply that Margaret had *'shown no emotion'* at the imposition of the death sentence.

Following the verdict and the handing down of the death penalty, however, Margaret did something else which might call her sanity into question. She declined to exercise her right to appeal her verdict and sentence. It is almost unheard of for a condemned prisoner not to appeal and, in each of those very few cases where this has happened, the prisoner's mental stability and soundness of judgement was already in doubt. Even where there are no obvious grounds for appealing, most clear-thinking people would realise that lodging an appeal would at least buy them a few extra precious days of life. And Margaret did want those precious extra days.

Having been raised, mostly, as a Roman Catholic but never confirmed in that religion, faced now with the prospect of execution, Margaret decided she would like to undergo a Catholic confirmation ceremony. This was duly arranged and was scheduled for 16 January which, incidentally, was also Annie's thirty-third birthday. Margaret was looking forward to a day of spiritual reconciliation with her maker, whom she believed she was about to meet, followed by time spent celebrating her religious confirmation with the woman she loved.

Margaret also asked the prison authorities whether, on that special day, she might also be allowed to spend some moments alone with Annie, rather than under the stern and disapproving gaze of the prison warders. It came as a bitter disappointment to both Margaret and Annie, however, when it was announced that the execution would take place on 12 January.

Margaret wrote, via the prison authorities, to the Home Secretary asking for a stay of execution of just four days in order to experience these two important events. Her plea was turned down, however, as was her request to be granted time alone with Annie.

It must surely have occurred to Margaret that lodging an appeal would delay her execution, probably beyond 16 January. However, she did not appeal. Her judgement in this is clearly both questionable and incomprehensible. Was this not another indication that she might not be in her right mind?

The petition

If Margaret had no stomach for an appeal, however, her loyal friend Annie did. She obtained leave of absence from her work at Glendale's Yarns in Cloughfold and spent two days and nights walking around Rawtenstall begging passers-by for their signatures on a petition for the Home Secretary.

Glendale's management thoughtfully furnished her with paper and pencils for her purpose and also allowed her to go around her own workplace and seek signatures of her fellow employees. She toured all the local mills, workshops and public houses in her quest to save her friend from the hangman's noose. Despite her best efforts, however, she

117

managed to obtain just 163 signatures from a local population of over 26,000.

The petition was headed *'We, the undersigned, knew Margaret Allen and are aware of her peculiarities and respectfully request a reprieve to be granted.'* Sadly, the petition did not attract much sympathy or interest. It did, however, bring much verbal abuse Annie's way, and even some physical jostling. Annie's sister, Mrs Gladys Flood, and her mother, Mrs Annie Tattersall, campaigned with her for some of the time but, intimidated by the angry reactions of some of the locals, they eventually left Annie to it.

Annie had even received hate mail for her support of Margaret. One such letter, post-marked Ashton-under-Lyne, moved her to declare to reporters: *'I would like to know who sent it. They obviously did not agree with my work for a reprieve. I shall keep it* [the letter] *as a souvenir'.*

A royal reprieve?

Rawtenstall's Labour Party took up Annie's petition and managed to increase the number of signatures to 300. Rossendale's Labour MP, 65-year-old George Henry Walker, who was strongly opposed to capital punishment, also wrote personally to the Home Secretary pleading for a reprieve. The 'royal reprieve', as it was known, was something of a misnomer. Though it would be granted or denied in the name of the monarch, it was actually decided by the Home Secretary alone. The reigning monarch did not really have any say in the decision.

The Home Secretary in 1948 was Walker's fellow Labour politician and trade unionist, 66-year-old James Chuter Ede. A Surrey-born and Cambridge-educated family man, he had been very active within the National Union of Teachers and had served the wartime Coalition Government as Parliamentary Secretary to the Board of Education. Given this background, it was unsurprising, that, during his tenure as the longest-serving Home Secretary of the twentieth century (1945-51), he would concern himself primarily with issues relating to *young* offenders.

In April 1948, it had been Sydney Silverman, the Labour MP for Nelson and Colne, who had tabled the bill to suspend the death penalty for five years, and the majority of MPs had voted in favour of that bill. Although the House of Lords subsequently threw out the bill and overturned the suspension, Chuter Ede had nevertheless signed off on a new Criminal Justice Act in July of 1948. However, this legislation, too, would focus mainly on young offenders.

The new act would abolish hard labour, penal servitude and the whipping of offenders, but would have no effect upon the commutation of death sentences, other than to define the legal implications of a royal pardon. Capital punishment, therefore, was still on the statue books. The act had also recommended the establishment of correctional institutions for young offenders rather than sending them to prisons.

Some politicians and members of the public had reacted to the act by accusing Chuter Ede of 'going soft' on criminals. However, if George Walker had expected his fellow Labour MP to 'go soft' on hanging a woman, he was to be disappointed. Chuter Ede's written reply was as follows:

'I am sorry to say that, after having carefully considered all the circumstances of the case, and having caused special inquiry to be made into Miss Allen's mental condition, I regret that I have not been able to find any grounds which would justify me in advising the King to interfere with the due course of justice.'

More pleas for clemency

The Rawtenstall Labour Party pressed Walker to make further representation to the Home Secretary, and he duly wired a further plea on his own behalf and that of the Labour Party membership, but to no avail.

As the eve of the execution approached, another appeal was received from a Middlesex clergyman. A 42-year-old bachelor, the Reverend Austin Lee, vicar of St Stephen's parish in Hounslow and author of several crime thrillers, petitioned Buckingham Palace direct. He also sent a telegram to the chief warder at Strangeways Prison calling upon him to resign *'rather than degrade all citizens of this country by hanging a woman'*.

A more regular campaigner against capital punishment was the wealthy, flamboyant and larger-than-life Mrs Violet Van der Elst. Born plain Violet Anne Dodge, daughter of a coal porter and a washer woman, Violet had worked as a scullery maid until, aged seventeen, she had met and married Henry Arthur Nathan, who was a civil engineer and thirteen years her senior. This marriage had enabled the resourceful Violet to develop a range of cosmetics, including 'Shavex', a brush-less shaving cream for men. This success of this product in particular had made Violet's fortune.

Having been widowed in 1927, a few months later Violet had married a Belgian, Jean Van der Elst, and the couple lived in great comfort at Harlaxton Manor in Lincolnshire, which they renovated and re-named Grantham Castle. By the time she was widowed for a second time, just seven years later, Violet had developed a strong social conscience and she now began to devote her energies and fortune to campaigning against capital punishment, which she decried as inhumane and barbaric. She even published a book, 'On the Gallows', which reflected her views on judicial execution.

It was Mrs Van der Elst's practice to drive her Rolls Royce up outside any prison on the day of an execution, step out into the crowd and, with the aid of a loudhailer, make a very vocal protest. A thorn in the side of the authorities, she was usually moved on, sometimes quite roughly, and was occasionally arrested for disturbing the peace.

She would sometimes hire aeroplanes and have the pilots swoop low over the prisons, trailing behind them banners displaying suitable words of protest. She would also hire men with sandwich boards bearing similar slogans and have them walk amongst the crowds. At other times, she would have a band play a death march outside the prison. Margaret Allen's execution would not be exempted from Violet's protesting presence.

Though the number of Rawtenstall folks willing to put their name to a petition to save Margaret was woefully small, requests for mercy came in from various groups and individuals around the country, including one from the citizens of the small community of Neston and Parkgate in The Wirral, Cheshire.

There were quite a few disparate voices raised in supplication, even though Margaret's own voice was not amongst them. However, few people really expected that, in the aftermath of so many war deaths and in a new climate of post war healing and recovery, the execution of a woman would actually go ahead. Tragically, though, there was to be no reprieve.

Chapter 12– The Execution

'The execution was done humanely and expeditiously,' – D.F. Eastcott, Medical Officer, Strangeways Prison, speaking of the hanging of Margaret Allen.

'It is not easy to die like that, but the fortitude of a woman comes through,' – Albert Pierrepoint, speaking of Margaret's execution.

Once the trial was over and the verdict handed down, Margaret's status changed from that of remand prisoner to condemned convict and she was moved into Strangeways' condemned cell, where she was watched over day and night by prison wardresses. She was never left alone, and the lights were kept on, albeit dimmed, all night so that she might not conspire to cheat the hangman by committing suicide.

As a condemned convict, she now had her own clothing taken away and was required to wear regulation prison uniform. To a woman who had enjoyed wearing uniforms, this might not have been an unwelcome imposition. To her horror, however, this particular uniform comprised a woman's blue-striped frock, knickers, brassiere, suspender belt, stockings and court shoes. How humiliating this must have been for someone who believed themselves male and who had worn men's clothing for almost all of their adult life.

Margaret pleaded to have her own clothes returned to her and begged to be allowed to meet her maker wearing her man's suit, but this modest and harmless request was denied. If the distress of facing death by hanging were not enough, Margaret was to continue to suffer the misery of being in the wrong body and now also the indignity of being in the wrong clothing. Thus, the last vestiges of her masculine identity were denied her.

Margaret had only one visitor whilst in prison, and that was her faithful friend Annie. Annie's final visit to the prison was on the afternoon of 11 January, the day before the execution. Margaret tried to put a brave face on, telling Annie she was looking forward to a 'last supper' of chicken, washed down with a bottle of beer. Notwithstanding the omnipresence of the wardresses, the two friends held each other in a tearful embrace. Theirs must have been a truly sad and difficult parting. Indeed, some sources relate that poor Annie fainted from shock on her way out of the prison gates.

Later that evening, as Margaret sat in the condemned cell on what would be her last evening on earth, her thoughts were of her only friend. Whilst Albert Pierrepoint and his assistant Harry Kirk were in the hang house nearby, rehearsing their gruesome procedures by dropping a weighted sandbag at the end of the executioner's rope, Margaret was writing her last letter to kindly Annie. This was a registered letter which Annie would not receive until after Margaret was dead and buried. Margaret wrote:

'Just a few lines to thank you and your family for all you have done for me. I cannot put into writing how I feel but thank you once again for making my last few hours happy by holding on to me. Don't forget what I said to you this afternoon to look after yourself. I can't say any more but God bless you all. Goodbye with love.'

Enclosed with the letter was Margaret's will. On a single sheet of prison notepaper, she had written: *'I, Margaret Allen, wish to leave all my personal property to Annie Cook.'* The sum total of Margaret's personal property was actually contained within the registered envelope. It comprised a pair of men's cufflinks, a ring, a cigarette lighter, a small crucifix, a photograph of Margaret's late mother and some loose change amounting to four shillings and five pence halfpenny[40]. These were the items which had been in Margaret's possession when she was arrested

---

[40] Worth just £7.24 nowadays.

and which had accompanied her into prison. Any clothing, furniture and other belongings left behind at 147 Bacup Road, and presumably also the money in her savings account, would be sequestered by Margaret's creditors.

During Annie's final visit, Margaret had made one last request of her dear friend. She asked Annie not to come to the prison for the execution the following morning, but to go instead to the corner of Kay Street and the Bacup Road, to the spot where they had so often met. Margaret asked that, at the appointed hour of nine o'clock, Annie should be standing at that corner of Kay Street, at their special spot, and should just stand there for a while and think of her.

Margaret assured Annie that, at the moment when the hangman would pull the trap, causing her to plunge to her death, her spirit would no longer be in Strangeways Prison. Instead, she would be up at the corner of Kay Street, looking down on her beloved Annie. Tearfully, Annie promised faithfully that she would indeed carry out Margaret's last wish.

When Margaret's last day on earth dawned, she awoke in an irritable mood. Perhaps it was that same irritable mood she had been experiencing when she had murdered Nancy Chadwick and which now prompted her to decline the condemned prisoner's last breakfast that she had requested the day before. Angrily, she told the wardress she would not eat the breakfast. She added *'if I'm not having it, then no-one else is having it!'* and she violently swept aside the tray of scrambled eggs, toast and tea, and sent it crashing to the cell's stone floor.

Was this just her menopausal mood kicking in once again? Or perhaps her anger was prompted by the final awful indignity the prison staff had, that morning, forced her to endure. Prison regulations stipulated that female prisoners about to be hanged must wear special underwear – stiff, padded canvas drawers. This was because of the likelihood of this violent method of execution causing the involuntary expulsion of a woman's reproductive organs, or, as is thought to have been the case with the 1923 hanging of Edith Thompson, causing the aborting of a foetus the prisoner was unaware she was carrying.

As Margaret was forced to step into this hideous canvas garment, doubtless she felt her humiliation was now complete. Despite the revulsion this caused her, and in spite of her outburst and understandable agitation at the prospect of imminent death, as soon as Pierrepoint and

Kirk came to lead her swiftly to the hang house, she gave no further trouble but meekly and obediently complied with their instructions.

Outside the prison, a crowd of around two thousand people stood in awed silence – silence, that is, save for Violet Van der Elst's strident and theatrical protests against capital punishment, hooted angrily through a loudspeaker. Meanwhile, within those high, soot-darkened brick walls, Margaret Allen walked stoically to the scaffold. Hers had not been an easy or pleasant life. Her death, too, would be unpleasant and brutal. Yet the prison chaplain would later remark that she met her death more bravely than any of the men he had ever witnessed being hanged.

Meanwhile, back in Rawtenstall, Annie was keeping her promise. Supported by her sister Gladys, and with her head held high, she walked to what had been her and Margaret's happy trysting place. As the hangman carried out his gruesome duty, Annie stood at the corner of Kay Street and Bacup Road, trembling, weeping and thinking of her 'Bill'.

Across the street, a crowd of some thirty or forty people stood and watched, some of them callously jeering. When the clock at St Mary's had finished chiming away the final moments of Margaret's difficult life, a devastated Annie and her sister made their way across to the church, where they knelt and prayed for the repose of Margaret's eternal soul.

Violet van der Elst's (centre) is the only truly sad face outside Strangeways Prison on the morning of 12 January 1949. (Photo unattributable).

124

Kay Street today, where it meets the Bacup Road, where Margaret would regularly meet her only friend, Annie, and where, on 1 January 1949, Annie kept her sad vigil. (Author's photo).

Chapter 13 – The Aftermath

'The circumstances under which he had been living lately had been such as to cause his mind gradually to become unhinged' – Coroner K.H. Rowland.

A tragic suicide

Nancy Chadwick was the victim in this affair, but she would not be the only victim. It seems her employer, 82-year-old John Edward 'Paddy' Whittaker, could not face the prospect of living without the housekeeper who had so closely controlled his life. Nor did he relish the prospect of giving evidence in court as the police had warned him he must do. He may also have been disheartened by the difficulties he would now have accessing his life savings which Nancy Chadwick had deposited in an account under her own name.

On 16 September 1948, a couple of weeks after the arrest of Margaret Allen, and two and a half months before the trial, Paddy had walked unsteadily out of his house and crossed the fields at Hall Carr. Less than a mile from his home he came to a lodge – a large reservoir of water for industrial use. It was here that he drowned himself.

His next-door neighbour, Mrs Jane McCullough, told the inquest into his death that Paddy had been in failing health and had often said he might take his own life. Recently, she said, he had told her about the summons to attend court, but said he could not face it. He had repeated

126

this to Mrs McCullough just as he was leaving his house on the day of his death and he had left her with the parting comment: *'I don't think I'll come back'*.

The verdict at the inquest was *'suicide whilst the balance of his mind was disturbed'*. Coroner K.H. Rowland added *'the circumstances under which he had been living lately had been such as to cause his mind gradually to become unhinged'*. Ironically, a similar conclusion might have been drawn from the recent circumstances of Margaret Allen's life, had she committed suicide instead of murder.

Another reluctant witness

Another victim of the affair was Strangeways' prison chaplain, the Reverend Joseph Walker, who was most disturbed by witnessing Margaret's execution. Four months later, he would tell a further royal commission on capital punishment that witnessing the hanging of Margaret Allen had caused him to suffer three heart attacks in fairly quick succession.

He told the commission:

'she was well prepared and behaved like a man. In fact, she had more guts than most men I have seen… the woman had plenty of grit, but I felt the whole thing was bestial and brutal'.

He impressed upon the commission his firm view, having himself witnessed the execution of five men without adverse effect upon himself, that the particular experience of seeing Margaret Allen executed had persuaded him that no woman should ever be hanged.

Walker said the execution of Margaret Allen had taken its toll on his health and on the health of others who had witnessed it. He added that, a year after the execution, one of the prison officials had told him he had *'never felt fit since the thing happened'*. Walker said also that even the normally cheerful governor of Strangeways, Mr C.T. Cape, had confided in him that, whenever he knew a woman was to be hanged, for two weeks beforehand he found himself unable to smile.

Governor Cape would continue to take a keen interest in the treatment and fate of prisoners. On 3 February 1949, just three weeks after Margaret's execution, Cape presented to the Manchester branch of the Medico-Legal Society a paper entitled 'The Purpose of Imprisonment

127

in England and Wales' which recommended a series of improvements with regard to the treatment of criminals.

The Reverend Walker had demanded of the Royal Commission members in May 1950:

'how many of you have seen a woman executed? The people who sit in the court give their verdict and their judgement, but the people who see the execution are the prison governor, chaplain, doctors and prison officers. I went into the prison service without any definite view on hanging. I have come out of it with the definite view that a woman should not be hanged – after seeing [just] *one woman hanged.'*

Walker emphasised the particular suffering experienced by condemned prisoners whilst awaiting execution, but said he also felt a sense of the suffering their deaths would cause their families. Walker said he would be a much happier man if he were allowed to slip a sleeping draught to the prisoner the night before the hanging, so that the prisoner would never more wake. The disturbing experience of seeing Margaret Allen hanged, and his consequent illness, had caused Walker to quit the prison chaplaincy and to take up instead a post as vicar in the quiet rural parish of Tushingham in Shropshire.

The stalwart campaigner

As expected, professional campaigner Mrs Violet Van der Elst had turned up as usual, clad in black mourning dress, to protest outside the prison on the morning of Margaret's execution. Again, as usual, this had been to no avail. Undaunted, the valiant Violet would never give up her quest and, despite the gradual loss of her fortune, would attend several more executions until, in 1965, she would see the death penalty finally abolished. The following year, aged 84, and by now impoverished but with her life's goal accomplished, she passed away. Towards the end of her life, she would declare that she had *'made two fortunes and lost five'*. It would be good to think, however, that she died happy in the knowledge that she had seen the end of capital punishment in Britain and had played her part in achieving that end.

The Home Secretary is unmoved

Chuter Ede was seemingly unmoved either by Margaret's plight or by the modest petition to spare her life. Executing a woman seemed to cause him no anguish whatsoever. Indeed, she would not be the last woman to hang in England and Wales.

The 1955 execution of Ruth Ellis would attract much more widespread protest and a petition containing fifty thousand signatures, although it would be Chuter Ede's successor as Home Secretary, Gwilym Lloyd George, who would reject this. In contrast to Margaret's execution, the hanging of this notorious, platinum blonde nightclub manageress would provoke significant public reaction.

This was perhaps due to the people's revulsion at the execution of a woman, rather than because of any doubt about Ellis's guilt. After all, the killing of Ellis's lover had been a clear case of pre-meditated murder, as evidenced by the use of a gun. So why were the public not equally revolted at Margaret's execution for an unpre-meditated killing? Was it, perhaps, because they did not view her as a woman?

There is now little doubt that the reason Ruth Ellis was not reprieved was because of another kind of revulsion; the abhorrence felt by the mainly male establishment over Ellis's lifestyle, for her occupation at the time was not considered respectable and, moreover, she had occasionally been reduced to making a living by prostitution.

Once out of office, however, Chuter Ede would undergo a surprising change of opinion about capital punishment. This *volte face* would not be influenced by the hanging of women, however, but by the executions of two men whose cases would attract much disquiet over the question of their guilt and the morality of *wrongly* executing someone.

The first of these would be the semi-literate Timothy Evans, hanged in 1950 for the murder of his infant daughter Geraldine, after Chuter Ede had declined a reprieve. Following the execution, it would be learned that the main witness against Evans, Reginald Christie who lived in the same house as the Evans family, was a serial killer who had in fact murdered Evans' wife Beryl, as well as his own wife and several other women.

Christie's subsequent conviction, and the unlikely possibility of there being two stranglers living in the same house, would eventually persuade the authorities of Evans' innocence of the killing of his daughter. In 1966, after much campaigning, Timothy Evans would receive a posthumous pardon.

The second case was that of the illiterate and epileptic Derek Bentley who had been deemed 'mentally unfit' for national service, but who, in 1953, would be considered sufficiently mentally fit to be hanged for his alleged complicity in the shooting of a policeman. Despite strong doubts over Bentley's ability to understand the consequences of his actions, and the ambiguity of his having exhorted his partner in crime to 'let him have it' when the policeman demanded the gun be handed over, Chuter Ede's successor as Home Secretary, David Fyfe Maxwell, would refuse to grant a reprieve. It would be forty years before Bentley would be pardoned, and a further five years before his conviction would be quashed.

These two executions and the related campaigns which continued into the 1960s would actually do more to achieve abolition than would all the many hours of endless parliamentary debate. Soon after the hanging of Bentley, Chuter Ede would begin to have severe misgivings about the soundness of Bentley's and Evans' convictions.

His conscience disturbed by the possibility of awful and irretrievable miscarriages of justice, he would now declare himself staunchly opposed to the death sentence and his was one of many voices demanding a Royal commission on Capital Punishment. That commission would take an overly long time but would finally present its conclusions in 1955.

This commission would again suggest suspension of hanging whilst capital punishment was under re-consideration, but, again, it would be rejected. Ede and others would persevere, however, and would submit the proposal for parliamentary debate yet again. This time it would pass.

1965 saw the eventual triumph by the abolitionists over the retributionists and the ending of judicial execution (for all but four rare offences: espionage, high treason, piracy with violence and arson in the royal dockyards). The 1998 Human Rights Act and the Crime and Disorder Act would see capital punishment abolished absolutely.

Chuter Ede has been credited with achieving numerous reforms to the criminal justice system and he was created Baron Chuter-Ede of Epsom in 1964. He even lived to see the partial abolition of judicial hanging just before he passed away in November 1965. These reforms were, of course, too late to save Margaret Allen.

Margaret is not forgotten

The execution of Margaret Allen was still affecting some individuals almost two decades after the event. In March 1968, a woman signing herself 'Mrs D.L.' wrote a passionate letter to the magazine 'Arena Three'[41]:

> '*Thirty-seven years ago, I knew Margaret Allen who, in January 1949, was hanged for being a lesbian, and I weep for her every January. The murder she committed was an insane one. But for the intolerance of her deviance, she would have been reprieved. The petition for her reprieve was circulated in an area of 60,000 population; it received 361 signatures, most of them by cripples and elderly people who remembered her as the kindest bus conductress on the route. Only a few weeks ago, I had evidence of the fact that to this day this intolerance of her memory continues[42].*
>
> *I remember her as a happy, laughing tomboy of twenty-one. It is for me peculiarly horrible to know that 'public opinion' first succeeded in driving her insane, then in ensuring her extermination and is largely unchanged in that locality.*'

The identity of the letter writer, who claimed to have known Margaret when the latter was aged twenty-one to thirty-one, is unknown.

The 'poodle' remembers

As for Annie, how did the execution of her best friend (and possibly her lover) affect her? In their book, Huggett and Berry stated that Annie had determined to leave Rawtenstall after the execution and they implied they had found it necessary to track her down to a different location. However, this was not so.

When in January 1955 they trekked through that blizzard to seek her out, Annie was still living in the Clough Fold area, just a few hundred yards from Margaret's former home. In fact, she had never left the area and never would. Most of the townsfolk of Rawtenstall knew Annie by sight. One local resident, and even one of Annie's own relatives, both say she was sometimes referred to, derisively perhaps, as 'Poodle Annie' (presumably suggesting she was considered to be Margaret's tame pet).

---

[41] 'Arena Three' was a British monthly publication founded in 1964 by Esme Langley and Diana Chapman, and written by and for homosexual women. It was published up until 1972 by the Minorities Group.

[42] Intriguingly, she does not state what this 'evidence' was, though it might have been the dredging up of the story by the press when 137 Bacup Road was earmarked for demolition.

Despite this, Annie stayed. Either she was unaware of, or she chose to ignore, continuing gossip about her association with an executed murderess.

As they had promised, Huggett and Berry revealed neither her location nor her personal circumstances in their book. Of course, this may have been to protect her from approaches by other writers or journalists who might steal a march on them. There was much press interest in executions at this time since the issue of capital punishment was undergoing intense debate.

Margaret had bequeathed to Annie her pitifully few worldly goods and Huggett and Berry asked if they might see these. However, Annie said she had not kept them. She said she had even thrown away the photograph of Margaret's mother, Alice. This may have been true, or she may indeed have kept the photo but did not want to show it to the writers in case they pressed her to let them publish it. We may be certain Margaret would not have wanted that.

What became of Annie?

Most surprisingly, perhaps, just five months after Margaret's execution, 33-year-old Annie married for a second time. The groom was 38-year-old bachelor Thomas Francis Beckett, a cotton worker from Preston. Annie's sister Gladys was one of the witnesses to the marriage which took place at Haslingden Register Office on 22 June 1949.

However, this marriage, like her first, would end in divorce. When Tom Beckett was to pass away some thirty-seven years later, his death would be registered by the warden of the sheltered housing complex in Preston where Tom had, for some years, occupied a single person's flat.

Seven years on from the execution, in August 1956, Annie, by then aged forty, married husband number three. She was living at 8 Queen Street, Cloughfold, when she wed another cotton worker. Her new husband was, in fact, her lodger, 55-year-old bachelor William Henry Hornby. It was still common for many working class single householders to take in lodgers to assist with the rent.

Annie and Billy Hornby next moved to 108 Fall Barn Crescent, a pleasant stone-built, end of terrace house with views of the hills, and a new lodger, Tommy Carr, came to occupy their second bedroom. A relative remembers Billy Hornby as being a very kind man, albeit that he had a pronounced deformity of the spine.

On 14 February 1977, Billy Hornby passed away at home. His death was registered by his widow, Annie. Just eight weeks after Hornby's funeral, however, Annie, now aged sixty-one, wed husband number four – her current lodger, Tommy Carr. Both the bride and the groom – a 59-year-old divorced rubber worker – gave their place of residence at the time of their marriage on 22 April 1977, as Annie's marital home, 108 Fall Barn Crescent.

On the face of it, it would seem that this marriage was contracted with an unseemly degree of haste, but again, it seems Annie was already well acquainted with the groom, since they shared a house. This being a register office marriage, it was not necessary for the couple to wait three months whilst banns were read, as would have been the case with a church wedding. Once again, however, a lodger had moved from the spare room into Annie's master bedroom.

Annie did not marry or divorce again and, when she passed away aged seventy-three on 12 December 1989 at Rossendale General Hospital, it was a health worker, rather than a relative, who registered the death and gave Annie's occupation as 'widow of Tom Carr, maintenance engineer (retired)'.

Annie died from cardio respiratory arrest and severe chronic obstructive airways disease, common conditions amongst cotton workers, which work Annie did all her life. These are also conditions common amongst heavy smokers, which Annie also was. Sadly, none of her family members still alive today possesses a photograph of Annie.

So, the question which is still uppermost in the minds of the more morbidly curious – whether Annie's relationship with Margaret Allen was a physical one – still remains open to conjecture. The fact that she married four men during her lifetime might be evidence enough for some that Annie was heterosexual. However, for all the husbands she had, Annie never had any children, and it may be that her marriages were entered into for economic reasons and for company, rather than out of a need to satisfy a heterosexual nature.

Did Margaret rest in peace?

As an executed criminal, Margaret Allen was buried within the precincts of Manchester's Strangeways Prison. There was no grave or other memorial, of course. Even had there been, Annie would not have been permitted to visit it. There was, therefore, no graveside at which Annie might have wept; no headstone against which she might have placed flowers from time to time. Margaret's mortal remains were destined to lie forever in a darkened corner of Strangeways' precincts; a place where the sun did not reach and no-one ever walked for fear of aggrieved ghosts.

In 1991, however, forty-two years after her execution and burial, Margaret's remains, along with those of sixty-two other executed prisoners, were exhumed to make way for extension work at the prison. The disinterred remains were cremated at Blackley Crematorium in north Manchester and, two years later, the ashes were buried in two large plots in the adjoining cemetery. Only forty-five of the sixty-two sets of remains, Margaret's amongst them, were able to be identified.

The date of Margaret's re-burial is recorded as 2 April 1993, more than three years after Annie had passed away. It is not known where Margaret's remains had lain during the intervening two years following the cremation, nor is it known why they were not buried immediately.

Here also, there is no headstone, just a basic plot number marker. No-one visits the spot where Margaret's mortal remains now rest. No-one leaves flowers. Few people are even aware that anyone at all lies in these unmarked plots and nor do they know what fate befell them. Annie, too, has no memorial, for, in the absence of any immediate family member, her simple cremation was arranged by staff at Rossendale hospital where, in 1989, she had passed away.

Annie had spent her final few years living alone in a modern and comfortable old person's terraced bungalow at 25 Hall Carr Road, Rawtenstall. Her final home was situated a little way above the Bacup Road, less than a mile from Clough Fold where Annie was born, and from the scene of the brutal killing which had led to Margaret's equally brutal death. In fact, throughout her life, Annie had never lived more than a mile from Margaret's home at 137 Bacup Road. One wonders if she had watched that property being demolished in 1972 and how she felt about its destruction.

In the forty years following Margaret's tragic fate, and notwithstanding Annie's four marriages, did Annie continue to remember Margaret, the good friend whom she had loved, supported, lost and mourned? I feel certain that she did.

The rear of Weaver's Cottage today, showing where 137 Bacup Road once stood. Margaret's front door would have been just to the right of the fence, marked now by a shrub, and the coal place, where Nancy's body was kept, is now marked by the paved area to the right of that. The Irwell is over in the distance on the left, just in front of the large trees. (Author's photo).

The Weaver's Cottage, formerly the loom shop, as seen from beyond the Irwell today. The railway, signal box and Fall Barn Crossing are all gone now and new houses straddle the hills of Margaret's horizons. (Author's photo).

POSTSCRIPT

The climate in which Margaret Allen was tried and sentenced to death was one which was averse to homosexuality. The population had been greatly depleted by war and so marriage and childbirth were officially encouraged. In her book[43], criminology lecturer Anette Ballinger asserts that *'the post-war climate in Britain was extremely hostile to gay men and lesbian woman, with prosecutions for [male] homosexuality reaching a peak in 1953.'*[44]

Ballinger also quotes the Catholic professor Thomas V. Moore,[45] writing in 1945, who advised that homosexuality was *'an acquired abnormality and propagates itself as a morally contagious disease.'* Moore warned that *'the growth of a homosexual society in any country is a menace ... to the welfare of the state.'*

Of course, Moore was writing of male homosexuality, because lesbianism was rarely acknowledged. Although lesbian acts were never made a criminal offence in England and Wales, historically, attitudes towards openly lesbian women, or those perceived to be lesbians, were every bit as hostile as those expressed towards homosexual men.

This was also an era in which the poor, especially poor women, did not have a voice. Ballinger writes that most women executed in England and Wales between 1900 and 1950 came from a background of abject poverty. Being poor, as well as seeming to be of ambiguous gender, Margaret had little chance of attracting public sympathy and support.

Following both world wars, the inevitable absence of marriageable men made it a little easier for unmarried lesbians or transgendered women to give the impression of being single by virtue of circumstances, rather than by choice.

However, women who openly chose to dress as men in order to make a statement of their sexuality, or of the gender with which they identified, often attracted prejudice and abuse. This certainly seems to have been the case in respect of Margaret Allen. But how has the world changed since Margaret's day? The honest answer is – very little.

---

[43] 'Dead Woman Walking: Executed Women in England and Wales 1900-1950'
[44] There had been 82 prosecutions for homosexuality in 1938 increasing to 3,305 in 1953.
[45] Author of 'The Pathogenesis and Treatment of Homosexual Disorders' 1945

In 1958, the Daily Express 'outed' the aristocratic Laurence Michael Dillon. Born Laura Dillon, he is believed to have been the UK's first beneficiary of female-to-male gender reassignment surgery. Although, as a man, he had qualified in medicine and had published several worthy medical books, the press exposure forced this decent, professional man to flee to India, where he lived as a religious hermit until his premature death at the age of forty-seven in 1962.

In 1957, publication of the Wolfenden Report would lead to the introduction, in 1967 and 2003, of new sexual offences legislation which would, in stages, decriminalise male homosexuality in England and Wales and define the age of male consent. Similar legislation would follow a little later in Scotland and Northern Ireland. Thus, there was a gradual legal acceptance of homosexuality. Public attitudes, however, were not so quick to change.

In passing the 1967 act, Home Secretary Roy Jenkins had summed up the establishment's attitude to homosexuality in that decade when he said *'those who suffer from this disability carry a great weight of shame all their lives'*. Today, however, homosexuality is no longer considered a disability but rather a natural disposition.

Did the difficult life and gruesome death of Margaret 'Bill' Allen do anything to change the world? Seventy years on, if she were alive today, would her life be any different? Would her day-to-day existence still be so awful that it would drive her to the point where she would kill someone? After all, today's world is a different place, isn't it? We no longer hang women or men. We are more liberal now. Our egalitarian society has moved on from intolerance, through acceptance, to actually valuing diversity. Moreover, we are nowadays more aware and understanding of mental illness and more successful at treating it. So, we now live in better times, don't we?

In 2015, the fiftieth anniversary of the abolition of capital punishment passed with little fanfare or comment. By contrast, in 2017 the fiftieth anniversary of the 1967 Sexual Offences Act was marked by events hosted by the Law Society and by several LGBT (Lesbian, Gay, Bi-sexual and Transgender) support groups. Several museums, including Manchester's People's History Museum, held exhibitions reflecting LGBT life.

Nowadays, sexual diversity and gender dysphoria are no longer classed as crimes or perversions. Our society is no longer shocked or repulsed by individuals who present as androgynous or who dress differently in order to assert their identity.

We no longer feel threatened by people who may challenge our perspective of what is 'normal'. We welcome freedom of expression and self-expression, so long as it hurts no-one. We do not persecute or attack people who dress in a way which reflects their faith, their gender, their affiliation to a football club or to a fashion trend which they feel identifies them – or do we?

Sad to relate, it would seem that intolerance is alive and well, not least in the Rossendale Valley. In 2008, a group of teenage boys viciously kicked to death a young woman. The youths murdered 22-year-old Sophie Lancaster purely because she chose to dress as a 'Goth'. This unprovoked attack took place in Bacup's Stubbylee Park, not far from Margaret Allen's childhood home. Sophie's similarly dressed boyfriend was also savagely assaulted but mercifully survived. Two of the teenagers were sentenced to life imprisonment and three were convicted of assault. Thus, the lives of several local families would never be the same again.

In 2013, in Accrington, just six miles from Rawtenstall, the community was shocked and distressed when a popular, 32-year-old primary school teacher committed suicide by taking poison. Lucy Meadows, who was born Nathan Upton, had announced to her employer her plan to transition from male to female during the school's long vacation. The school's head teacher had written in sensitive terms to the parents of children at the school, explaining why, the following term, Mr Upton would be returning as Miss Meadows. Most of the parents were sympathetic and accepting of Lucy Meadows' situation. However, at least one parent, who felt his children were too young to understand this issue, complained, and, somehow, the story was leaked to the more salacious press.

The Daily Mail in particular ran with the most offensive headline: *'he's not only in the wrong body, he's in the wrong job'*. Understandably hurt, Ms Meadows made a formal complaint to the Press Complaints Commission regarding this slur on her right and suitability to follow her vocation, but the newspaper's own response was ineffective to the point of insult. It was shortly after this that Miss Meadows killed herself. At the inquest into her death, the coroner hit out angrily at the 'ill-informed bigotry' of the press and singled out the Daily Mail journalist in particular for blame.

Even more recently, in February 2017, following months of incessant bullying at her Greater Manchester school, and having been spat at, drenched with water and kicked to the ground, an eleven-year-old transgender pupil was shot and wounded by a fellow pupil armed with a ball-bearing gun.

Leaving aside the verbal abuse and prejudicial treatment which transgendered individuals are still, in this 'enlightened' twenty-first century, obliged to endure, actual physical attacks upon them are on the increase. Moreover, UK charities claim that the rising level of unprovoked attacks on transgendered people is disproportionate to their numbers. Across the UK, violence against transsexuals has become so frequent and widespread that it now has its own name – Transphobia.

The 20 of November each year has been designated International Transgender Remembrance Day and is when people around the world come together to remember transgendered people who have lost their lives, either through suicide, medical mishaps or murder, as a result of their gender situation. Manchester Cathedral, for example, held a Transgender Remembrance Day service in November 2016.

In 2016, only twenty-six out of the forty-five UK police authorities responded to a Freedom of Information enquiry which sought figures on complaints of violence against transsexuals. Incomplete though their statistics were, where figures existed they revealed there had been a 170% increase in the reporting of transphobic hate crimes over the four-year period since the recording of this specific category of crime had begun. Such recorded complaints, which included threatening behaviour, sexual assaults and other types of violent harassment, had increased from 215 cases in 2011 to 582 in 2015.

Such an increase in reports might simply reflect a growing confidence on the part of the victims to come forward and complain. However, just fifteen police forces were able to supply prosecution rates for transphobic hate crimes during that period, and from these it was clear that, though complaints were greatly increased, successful prosecutions seemed to be falling, from twenty-two in 2014 to nineteen in 2015.

Though most police forces and their governing body the Home Office are slowly becoming aware of the vulnerability and rights of transsexuals, sadly, the Ministry of Justice, now in charge of prisons, seems lamentably slow to grasp the essential human issues. Following the suicides in 2015 of Joanne Latham and Vicky Thompson – two male-to-female transgendered offenders who, despite their protests, were held

140

in male prisons – the Government announced it would review its policy towards transgendered prisoners.

Before that review was held, however, Jenny Swift, another transwoman held in a male prison, also committed suicide in December 2016. At the time of writing, there are seventy transgendered people being held in British prisons. Not all are in prisons appropriate to the gender with which they identify.

As disturbed as we may be by the mental image of Margaret 'Bill' Allen spending her final miserable weeks on earth in a condemned cell and forced, against all the instincts of her nature and to her intense humiliation, to wear women's clothing, we can take very little comfort in the fact that it has taken a further seven decades for the treatment of transgendered prisoners to even be tabled for consideration by the relevant authorities.

ABOUT THE AUTHOR

Manchester-born Buckinghamshire resident Denise Beddows has a background in research, investigation and intelligence analysis. Having taken early retirement from a career which enabled her to work and play in twenty countries across four continents, she nowadays writes – both as Denise Beddows and as DJ Kelly – non-fiction, biographical fiction and screenplays. A member of the Society of Authors and the Society of Women Writers & Journalists, she regularly contributes articles to local, national and international press and journals, and is a volunteer researcher for several local history groups. A trained and experienced public speaker, she regularly gives talks on different topics to a variety of community groups and at literary festivals. She actively supports Chalfont St Giles Literary Festival.

Also by this author:
NON-FICTION:

Buckinghamshire Spies and Subversives by DJ Kelly

Buckinghamshire has a 600-year history of subversion, sedition and espionage. The county has been home to radical plotters, heretic hunters, agents provocateurs and informers. Two world wars brought spies, secret agents and saboteurs to the county. Many of our stately homes housed wartime code-breakers, eavesdroppers, boffins, intelligence chiefs and even Nazi officers. A surprising number of women spies were incarcerated here and the first use of covert surveillance photography was against local women.

> *'First class and utterly absorbing. Informative, sensitive and revealing. An excellent contribution to the history of British Intelligence and its development through the ages.'*
> – Mark Birdsall, Editor, Eye Spy Magazine.

> *'A different perspective on a surprisingly large amount of Bucks history ... offers a fascinating insight into people and events our ancestors' lives may have been affected by – whether or not they were aware of it.'*
> – Buckinghamshire Family History Society

*****

The Chalfonts and Gerrards Cross at War by DJ Kelly

Exploring the ways in which conflict throughout the ages – including two world wars – has affected the people, the way of life and even the landscape of our beautiful villages.

*****

The Famous and Infamous of the Chalfonts & District by DJ Kelly

The beautiful villages of the Chalfonts, Gerrards Cross, Denham, Fulmer and Hedgerley have long attracted people to settle. A surprising number of the area's residents have been famous. A few, however, have been downright infamous.

*****

FICTION:

A Wistful Eye – The Tragedy of a Titanic Shipwright by DJ Kelly

A novel based on the true story of the murder of the author's great grandmother Belle, and of the role played by her great grandfather William Henry Kelly in building the Titanic.

'A fascinating and thoroughly enjoyable read' – The Historical Novel Society

'A mighty fine achievement' – Family Tree Magazine

'Highly recommended' – The Belfast Titanic Society

'A captivating read' – Ulster Tatler Magazine

*****

Running with Crows – The Life and Death of a Black and Tan by DJ Kelly

A novel based on the true, but hitherto untold, story of William Mitchell, the only member of the British Crown Forces to be executed for murder during the Irish War of Independence. Was this in fact a tragic miscarriage of justice?

'An absolutely fascinating read' – Irish Evening Herald

'I heartily recommend this book' – West Wicklow Historical Society

'An excellent and well researched book' – Royal Irish Constabulary forum

*****

All are available in paperback online and from all good bookshops.

Lightning Source UK Ltd.
Milton Keynes UK
UKHW010034101120
373079UK00001B/99